The DP Professional's Guide to Writing Effective Technical Communications

The DP Professional's Guide to Writing Effective Technical Communications

J. VAN DUYN

*EDP Management Consultant
Adjunct Faculty Member
California State University, Sacramento*

A Wiley-Interscience Publication
JOHN WILEY & SONS
New York • Chichester • Brisbane • Toronto • Singapore

Copyright © 1982 by John Wiley & Sons, Inc.

All rights reserved. Published simultaneously in Canada.

Reproduction or translation of any part of this work beyond that permitted by Section 107 or 108 of the 1976 United States Copyright Act without the permission of the copyright owner is unlawful. Requests for permission or further information should be addressed to the Permissions Department, John Wiley & Sons, Inc.

This publication is designed to provide accurate and authoritative information in regard to the subject matter covered. It is sold with the understanding that the publisher is not engaged in rendering legal, accounting, or other professional service. If legal advice or other expert assistance is required, the services of a competent professional person should be sought. *From a Declaration of Principles jointly adopted by a Committee of the American Bar Association and a Committee of Publishers.*

Library of Congress Cataloging in Publication Data:

Van Duyn, Julia.
　The DP professional's guide to writing effective technical communications.

　"A Wiley-Interscience publication."
　Includes index.
　1. Technical writing.　2. Electronic data processing—Authorship.　I. Title

T11.V36　　　　808'.0666　　　81-15998
ISBN 0-471-05843-2　　　　　　AACR2

Printed in the United States of America

10　9　8　7　6　5　4　3　2

Preface

The primary objective of this book is to provide DP professionals a comprehensive, practical source of knowledge about one of the essential though somewhat neglected skills of the information industry: written communications. To emphasize its pragmatic approach, functional examples and sample applications illustrate the straightforward, step-by-step description of how to write effective technical presentations.

After the first chapter introduces the topics, Part I presents the basic tools and skills necessary for clear and succinct writing; Part II details how to write systems-related documents; Part III shows how to write successful technical proposals, explains how to write company manuals, and reveals how to write and sell technical articles.

This book is intended for DP managers, computer systems analysts, programmers, and auditors. It is also meant for college students whose curriculum of computer systems analysis and data processing would not be complete without being able to write useful, quality documents.

J. VAN DUYN

Loomis, California
March 1982

Contents

One	Introduction	1
PART I	BASIC TOOLS AND SKILLS OF WRITTEN COMMUNICATIONS	11
Two	Mechanics of Clear Writing	13

Basic Principles, 14
Write to Communicate, 17
Have a Purpose, 18
Use Direct, Uncomplicated Language, 18
Get to the Point, 19
Be Concise but Informative, 20
Use Personal not Impersonal Viewpoint, 20
Watch out for Acronyms and Initials, 21
Edit to Eliminate Complexity and Redundancy, 22

Three	Defining Your Target Readers	25

Reader-Oriented versus Product-Oriented Communications, 26
Who Is Your Target Audience?, 27
Aim at Your Reader's Interest Level, 28
Writing to and not for Management, 31
Writing to Peers, 33
Writing to Subordinates, 33
Writing to the Public, 33

Four	**Steps Prior to Writing**	35

Define the Project, 36
Gather Data, 37
Get the Most out of Interviews, 38
Check the Software by Using It, 42
Organize the Collected Data, 42
Sample Applications, 44
Determine Your Document's Personality, 47
Outline Your Material, 47
Summarize Your Subject, 50
Define the Layout and Content Standards, 50
Define the Layout and Format Standards, 50

Five	**Mechanics of Data Processing Graphics**	53

Charts, 54
Tables, 66
Exhibits, 74
Graphical Documentation, 76

PART II	**WRITING SYSTEM-RELATED DOCUMENTS**	87

Six	**Writing Effective Progress Reports**	89

Front Section, 90
Summary, 93
Introduction, 94
Discussion, 95
Conclusion, 95
Sample Application, 97

Seven	**Writing Usable Procedures**	103

Preliminary Steps/Considerations, 104
Final Copy, 107
Follow-Up/Updating Method, 107
Sample Applications, 108
Sign-Off/Approval, 109

Contents ix

Eight	**Writing the Systems Study**	123

Planning the Feasibility Study, 124
Investigating and Defining the Problems, 125
Identifying Existing Constraints, 125
Researching and Analyzing Possible Alternatives, 125
Developing a Solution, 125
Writing the Feasibility Study, 126
Sample Application, 129
Sample Design Specifications, 141

PART III	**WRITING OTHER TYPES OF TECHNICAL MATERIAL**	145
Nine	**Writing a Winning Technical Proposal**	147

The Small and Simple Proposal, 148
Sample Application, 152
The Large and Complex Proposal, 160
Sample Application, 164

Ten	**Writing Policy and Standards Manuals**	181

Policy Manuals, 182
Sample Application, 184
Standards Manuals, 186
Sample Applications, 188

Eleven	**Writing and Selling Technical Articles for Publication**	199

Preliminary Steps, 200
Sample Application, 202
Cover or Query Letter, 204
Sample Application, 207
Writing the Article, 211
Sample Application, 214

Index		215

The DP Professional's Guide to Writing Effective Technical Communications

Chapter One
Introduction

It is a well-known fact that the more adept some systems analysts, programmers, and other data processing (DP) professionals are in performing their work, the less effective they are in communicating with users, especially non-DP users.

Authorities who concern themselves with the human side of DP offer many theories about the communications problem that seems to permeate the field. Some say that the schools are to blame for emphasizing technical subjects and training. Others claim that the people attracted to this discipline are too involved solving technical problems, and consequently are not aware of the problems and requirements of non-DP users, especially users in the business world. Still others say that because DP professionals do not take the time and trouble to communicate with the marketplace, they are not solving the problems the customers are concerned with.

Marketing personnel, on the other hand, prove that DP professionals can learn to communicate. Thus presale systems analysts/systems engineers learn not to respond to customers' questions with raw technical, scientific, or statistical data. They convince the customers in simple, everyday language that their company has the ability to resolve the stated problem(s). Moreover, the DP marketing personnel also know that to communicate well he or she has to ask the right questions and do a great deal of listening.

It is interesting to note that after the presale DP marketing professional thoroughly understands the requirements and problems of the customer, he or she relays this information down to the technical level. And it is at this level that the DP facility systems analyst/designer or programmer/analyst designs or modifies the computer system or application for the customer.

Not surprisingly, DP professionals who rarely get involved with customers tend to have difficulties in communicating with non-DP users.

To help DP professionals master written communications, this book presents the basic tools and skills as well as flexible guidelines for producing effective technical presentations. In addition, since people learn style, format, and appropriate language by reading good documentation and then writing similar material, a large number of sample applications are included in the text.

HOW TO USE THIS BOOK

To facilitate finding specific information, the book is organized into three major sections. They are: 1. Basic Tools and Skills of Written Communications, 2. Writing System-Related Documents, 3. Writing Other Types of Technical Material.

PART I. BASIC TOOLS AND SKILLS OF WRITTEN COMMUNICATIONS

USE CRISP, DIRECT, UNADORNED LANGUAGE IN YOUR COMMUNICATIONS

a. *Mechanics of clear writing.* Whether writing a feasibility study, progress report, proposal, or any other communication, organize your material for greatest impact. This you can achieve by outlining your document; writing clearly and concisely; using simple yet vivid language; and aiming at a particular audience. The best technical presentations are written for a specific audience, for a specific purpose. Furthermore, in such documents the communicator is not trying to impress the reader with ostentatious words and phrases intermingled with technical jargon. The computer systems, operations, procedures, and the like are described in lucid, succinct language, using an informal tone. Formal, stilted language and style are a thing of the past. It is crisp, direct, and unadorned language that is used today, especially in the DP field. That doesn't mean, however, that you can sacrifice relevant information, accuracy, and clarity for brevity.

Purpose is another essential component of effective writing. It gives substance and cohesiveness to the document.

The attitude of the person writing the material is as important as the presentation having a purpose. If the

Part I. Basic Tools and Skills of Written Communications

writer's attitude is to serve the readers; if the person thinks of himself or herself as a communicator first and a DP professional second, then he/she is going to communicate well and produce a useful document.

A common pitfall of DP professionals is using undefined acronyms and initials in their communications. While the originator may know the definitions of all the acronyms and initials in the presentation, other DP personnel may not. And nontechnical readers surely have no idea of the meanings of those strange-looking words. Consequently, you will increase the reader's understanding of your material if you define each acronym and initial the first time you use it. In addition, it's a good idea to list all such items, even the simplest ones, in a glossary.

EDIT FOR EFFECTIVE PRESENTATION

After you have observed all the niceties of lucid, distinct writing, there is one final step: editing. Editing is crucial for producing useful, quality documents. When editing your communication, you should not only challenge every sentence to ensure that it gives valid information in the smallest number of simple words, but you should also check if your material flows smoothly from one line to the next, from one paragraph to another. And finally, you should verify that the effect of the presentation is consistent with your initial purpose.

CONSIDER YOUR READERS

b. *Defining your target readers.* To ensure a useful document, it's vital that the DP professional defines his/her readers and zeros in on the particular audience's basic needs and preferences. Technical communicators who don't relate to their readers produce their material in a vacuum. Perhaps it is this sort of dissociation that causes systems, programs, and procedures documentation to be treated as residual activity—an unpopular task to be put off until all "important" work has been completed. Much too often the result is NO documentation.

Simply put, whatever your writing project is, you must first study and analyze your potential readers. There are many levels of communications in the DP field, so be sure to define the particular audience you want to reach.

c. *Steps prior to writing.* The steps you take before beginning to write determine the quality and effectiveness of your final product. These preliminary activities include:

1. Defining and establishing the objective, scope, object audience, tentative schedule, and the cost of producing your document. The last step you do only if your firm uses the "charge out" system. In any case, these preliminary steps (detailed in Chapters 3 and 4) will give you a blueprint of the intended project, and make your actual writing task easier.

_{PROPER PRELIMINARY STEPS ARE THE BUILDING BLOCKS FOR USEFUL DOCUMENTS}

2. Gathering data in a systematic manner. This may be done in several ways. A couple of methods worth mentioning are the "top-down" and the "bottom-up" approaches described at length in Chapter 4. Whichever approach you use, however, it should include interviewing all persons who will be using your document(s): the DP staff, the non-DP staff, and the outside users, if the project involves a user's guide or other documentation for the customer.

3. Interviewing to collect information at the prime source. Please note, however, that, as explained in detail in Chapter 4, only well-planned interviews that include preparation of a list of relevant questions based on research will yield valid information.

ORGANIZE YOUR DATA ACCORDING TO PRIORITIES

4. Organizing the collected data according to the priorities that you have established in your objective (step 1). In other words, the sequence of arranging the collected data and information depends on what your purpose is and who is going to use your document. (For full explanation see Chapter 4.)

5. Determining the layout and content formats before you actually start writing. This is quite important, unless

Part I. Basic Tools and Skills of Written Communications 5

the company can provide you with established format standards.

ESTABLISH ATTRACTIVE LAYOUT AND CONTENT FORMATS

The layout format standards include definition of the type and color of paper, the type font, the width of the margins, and the color and thickness of the binders.

The content format standards should define how the title page, table of contents, and list of illustrations will be presented. An attractive content format can be achieved by liberal use of headings and illustrations.

OUTLINING YOUR MATERIAL CAN SAVE TIME AND EFFORT

6. **Outlining your communication** before you do any writing is as significant as preparing a list of questions before you interview anybody. An outline can help you to stick to your defined goal and be of substantial help in writing your document. Specifically, you are able to pick out any block of related information or module within your outline, write it, and not lose its place in the finished document. Also, you can move the blocks around, if it appears that a particular block of information would be more effective in a different section of your presentation. The three kinds of outlines are discussed and illustrated with samples in Chapter 4.

7. **Summarizing the content** of your communication on one page, if possible, is a valuable exercise in thinking through a project. It forces you to state your purpose and your subject clearly and concisely.

USE GRAPHICS TO GIVE YOUR DOCUMENT EYE APPEAL

d. *Mechanics of data processing graphics.* Graphics is an excellent tool for visually expressing ideas, theories, facts, corporate structures, flow of systems, flow of manual processing, and many other concepts. Graphics, whether drawn manually or produced via computer systems, can aid tremendously in explaining a complex computer system or technical subject to both DP and non-DP audiences.

In addition, graphics is used as a documentation device. Systems, programs, and processing can be graphically presented before, during, and after the design, development, and implementation of projects. The two graphical documentation methods discussed in Chapter 5 are: HIPO (Hierarchical Input Process Output) an IBM-originated documentation technique; and SADT (Structure Analysis and Design Technique), a documentation tool developed by Softech (The Software Technology Company). HIPO treats a system as a hierarchy of functions and subfunctions, presenting these activities at succeeding levels of detail. SADT, on the other hand, is a top-down, problem-definition-oriented technique that describes a system in terms of data diagrams and activity diagrams, and their relationships.

PART II. WRITING SYSTEM-RELATED DOCUMENTS

a. *Writing effective progress reports.* This excellent communication tool, when used properly, can save a lot of money and effort for the enterprise. Key ingredients of progress reports are:

1. An attractive, informative front section that consists of a title page, a table of contents, a list of illustrations (if it's a long report), and a summary.

> **DISTINCT PROGRESS REPORT SUMMARIES WILL BE NOTED BY MANAGEMENT**

The last item is more than an overview of the report. It provides management an accurate digest on the progress of a particular project. And perhaps just as important: it can, if it's well-written, arouse the interest of the executives, so that instead of "later" they will read the rest of the report immediately. This in turn will shorten the time the DP professional may have to wait for some sort of decision on the project, a not unusual occurrence.

2. An introduction that does not duplicate the summary. It states the period covered by the report, the actual progress (or lack of progress) with the assignment, AND the problems that were met. In short, the introduction addresses only major points of interest to management.

3. A discussion that (being the body of the progress report) provides a detailed account of the progress made. It also tells of the difficulties or problems, AND the potential problems that may be encountered. This is done

Part II. Writing System-Related Documents

without any elaborate excuses, and using a matter of fact tone.

4. **A conclusion** that not only sums up the essential points discussed in the body of the report, but also states the due date of the next report and the tasks expected to be performed in the next reporting period, if there is one.

WRITTEN PROCEDURES ENFORCE STANDARDS

b. *Writing usable procedures.* Clearly written, well organized, and (if appropriate) illustrated procedures are imperative for uniformity and efficiency of both manual and DP activities.

Producing functional procedures calls for:

1. **Establishing preliminary steps.** This includes studying existing documentation about the particular activity or process; observing at first hand the functions; and discussing the activity with personnel who are or will be involved in the procedures.

2. **Ensuring that the document's style, format, language, and level of information are not only appropriate for the specific procedures but helpful to the audience who will use the document.** Thus, to eliminate any possible misunderstanding about the technical terminology used in the procedures, include a glossary. Also, list the names and extension numbers of key staff personnel, so that people who are doing the procedures can get help quickly, if necessary. Finally, include a "Communicating and Operating Hints" section in the appendix, as well as additional sources of information for people who may want to learn more about the subject.

3. **Getting a sign-off/approval by the appropriate department manager.** This little formality will save you possible future problems or questions.

4. **Establishing an updating and follow-up method for the procedures.** Generally, a simple "Updating Log" form and a one-page "Follow-up" instructions will satisfy this requirement.

c. *Writing the systems study.* Systems studies is the collective name for feasibility studies, management re-

SYSTEMS STUDIES CAN BE FOR INTERNAL OR EXTERNAL USE

quirements planning studies, computer systems design specifications, and programming specifications, to mention a few. Generally, these documents are either reports for internal use or reports for the users (either within the enterprise or outside).

1. For internal use the systems studies are comprised of the following parts: front section (title page, table of contents, and list of illustrations), introduction (restatement of assignment), and discussion (statement of the problem, summary of present system, if there's one, and recommendation of a solution among several possible alternatives, based on data gathered and verified). And finally, cost of the recommended system, as well as its projected effectiveness and benefits for the enterprise.

Except for the front section, specifications, though they may be called systems studies, follow a different format. As the name implies, this type of document states precisely the particulars of management requirements, or the details of a computer system design or programs.

2. For the users the systems studies are often quite similar to those for internal use. If the users are not DP staff, however, the systems studies are more general in approach, using a minimum of technical terms.

PART III. WRITING OTHER TYPES OF TECHNICAL MATERIAL

The first section of Part III is devoted to a very important if often neglected subject in schools and technical writing seminars: technical proposals. Moreover, this section contains actual sample applications that can be used readily by the reader. Or, if that's not feasible, parts of these proposals can be adapted to fit the reader's particular needs.

a. *Writing a winning technical proposal.* This provides step-by-step procedures in preparing an effective technical proposal. If the proposal is well-written, meaningful and concise, has a spacious format with functional illustrations, is logically organized and easily referenced, and cost-attractive, it is likely to be a winner.

Part III. Writing Technical Proposals

WHEN WRITING A POLICY MANUAL IT'S IMPERATIVE TO GET MANAGEMENT'S APPROVAL AND THE GOOD WILL OF STAFF

b. *Writing policy and standards manuals.* In writing company manuals, whether it's a manual establishing corporate policy or standards and procedures, it is imperative to establish rapport not only with management but also with the staff for whom the documents are written. If you do, it will be much easier to get information from those people, and you will have much more success in having them accept and use your manuals. Thus, while management's approval is important, getting the cooperation of staff is essential. To achieve this, or at least go a long way toward that goal, assure the staff in words and in actions that you are working *with them and not against them.*

1. **Company policy manuals.** To write a useful policy manual that defines, establishes, and disseminates the information about the corporate policy within the enterprise, you should go through the same preliminary steps as in any other document. Once the required data have been gathered and organized, an outline prepared, and a sign-off/approval received from your manager, you are ready to write the manual. The document, in addition to the previously discussed front section (see Part II, a.1), includes: a foreword or preface (signed by top management), instructions for using and updating the manual when new/replacement pages are issued, and descriptions of the firm's policies as established by top management. These policies may cover job responsibilities, promotions, hiring and firing, vacations, training, communications protocols, development directions, and the like.

2. **Company standards and procedures manuals.** When writing company standards and procedures manuals, the preliminary steps are identical to those for the corporate policy manual. However, you may have to establish specific forms and styles that are appropriate to the particular manuals.

NOTE: Be careful that your instructions are detailed but not dogmatic, and that your illustrations are simple.

c. *Writing and selling technical articles for publication.* This section provides the distinctive steps that must be taken to write and sell technical articles for outside publications. Published examples show the types of articles that are bought by commercial technical magazines and newspapers. And because query letters are essential in selling articles to editors, sample query letters are also included in the text.

PART ONE
Basic Tools and Skills of Written Communications

PART ONE

Chapter Two
Mechanics of Clear Writing

While nobody expects proposals or training manuals to be on any best-seller list or even to be warm and exciting, they should be well-written. This means material that is organized systematically, paragraphs that flow smoothly from one to the other, and direct language that is devoid of clichés and technical jargon.

Consequently, if you organize your material for greatest impact, outline your presentation logically, and write clearly and economically, you will produce informative, easy-to-read document(s). In addition, if you communicate in second person instead of the impersonal third person—particularly when writing a user's guide—you can't miss producing a useful document. (You have to be careful, though, that you don't slip from friendly to imperative tone.)

Now incisive, well-organized, and informal writing that communicates ideas accurately doesn't just happen. To achieve clarity and succinctness—two essential ingredients of effective communication—you must ruthlessly cut your text until it's lean and spare. This is a lot of work, but the result is worth the effort.

A guide to clear writing follows.

1. BASIC PRINCIPLES

WRITE WITH DISCRIMINATION

Among the many elements of effective writing the least understood yet perhaps the most important is discrimination. The clearest, most forceful material is written with DISCRIMINATION, for a SPECIFIC AUDIENCE.*

First, the definition: discriminative writing means shunning redundancy; using adjectives and adverbs selectively; avoiding ambiguous words and phrases; using only active verbs; being consistent in the tenses; and varying the structure of sentences (subject-predicate-object continually makes for an uninteresting text).

SHUN VERBIAGE

a. **Redundant words and phrases** diffuse effective writing by inserting unnecessary material, or repeating the basic meaning of words they modify. Programmers, for example, will say: "When the system blew up, it totally demolished the program I was working on." Can demolition be other than total? Then there's the phrase often encountered in manuals, proposals, and textbooks: "refer back," when the first word would be sufficient. And how many times do you come across the phrase "facts and figures" when "data" would be quite adequate? Or, "The purpose of this chapter in the Systems Department Procedure Manual is directed toward establishing an understanding of the application, use, and administration of the BRT package." Wouldn't it be simpler to say, "This chapter explains the application, use, and administration of the BRT package"?

USE ADJECTIVES AND ADVERBS SPARINGLY

b. **Adjectives and adverbs** are most effective when used selectively. Overworked adjectives such as VERY useful (how useful is very?), GREAT wealth of material (how much is great wealth?), have no place in concise writing. Similarly, adverbs such as *highly* or *significantly*, when used improperly, as in *significantly* important item (how

---

*See Chapter 3 for detailed discussion of audience.

Basic Principles 15

can important be significant?), can be dead weight in a text.

c. **Ambiguous words and phrases** abound in technical materials. A case in point is a sentence taken from a feasibility study: "This implies a system that is thoroughly human factored." Besides taking the noun "factor" and inventing a new adjective, "factored," what does the phrase mean? If the designed system is for both data processing (DP) and non-DP people, the writer should say so.

DEFINE YOUR ACRONYMS

As for confusing words, how many people in the DP field know what *HASP, BASIC, JCL, BSAM, TSO, and many other acronyms mean without looking up the definition in a computer dictionary, unless the writer defines it the first time he or she uses it?

DON'T TURN YOUR VERBS INTO NOUNS

d. **Verbs** become ineffective if turned into nouns. Using a noun as a verb, and then propping it up with a weaker verb is also bad. For example, "We shall provide the development of a training curriculum," instead of "We will develop a training course." Or, "The establishment of standards and procedures is an essential factor in efficient data processing," instead of "Establishing standards and procedures is essential for efficient data processing."

In both of these first examples the verbs "develop" and "establish" are turned into the nouns "development" and "establishment," destroying their vitality.

ACTIVE VERBS EFFECT VIGOROUS WRITING

Active verbs make for interesting reading; passive verbs make your writing about as inviting as cold mashed potatoes. Consider the following paragraph taken from a technical field manual:

---

*See Section 8 of this chapter for definitions.

If initial settings of sense switches are to be changed from one run to another (but are to remain fixed for each individual case), modification of the program is recommended, so that it reads in a set of sense switch setting for each case.

While this sentence is technically correct, it could be improved. Here's the edited version:

To change the initial settings of sense switches from one run to another (but to ensure that they remain fixed for each individual case), modify the program to read the sense switch settings for each case.

Here's an outstanding example of a string of passive verbs, coupled with overblown adjectives and wrapped in false elegance:

GEM OF A SENTENCE

Action-oriented orchestration of innovative inputs, generated by escalation of meaningful ingenious decision-making dialog, focusing on viable intrastructure policy was the scenario of the meeting.

DON'T SWITCH TENSES

e. **If you start your communication in the present tense,** use the present tense throughout. Don't switch to the future or past tense in the middle of a sentence or paragraph. For example:

EXAMPLE

The minicomputer *provided* a solution to facilities that could not afford the larger systems. The minis *are* also used to distribute applications among various divisional and branch offices. This distribution processing *will* reduce cost, simplify software, and bring data processing under user control.

In this one short paragraph the writer started out in the past tense, went on to the present tense, and ended in the future tense.

f. **If you're presenting technical material,** in addition to communicating the needed information simply and succinctly, you should choose a format featuring plentiful headings and a liberal number of examples. Such techniques break the monotony of a straight text, and make the material more palatable to your readers.

2. WRITE TO COMMUNICATE

RELATE TO YOUR READER

If you want to communicate with your audience, you must think of yourself as a communicator first and a technical writer second. The simplest way of doing this is to become the "user," or at least try to imagine the sort of information the particular user would be looking for in the document you're writing. If you do, you will stop writing extravagant or tedious sentences to which no one can relate. Moreover, you will realize that to give the appropriate information to the programmers and analysts, for example, you must communicate in a different manner than to management, computer technicians, or the non-DP users. Again, it's distinction that makes the difference. And your finished copy will mirror this quality. Consider this example:

CASE IN POINT

A file is a collection of records treated as a unit. A data processing procedure is normally concerned with entire files of records. These files are placed on the input device, where the computer has access to them. To print and read a record from a file, one or more instructions in the program activate the input device and place the record in storage.

Compare the above text with:

A simple method of using files is to treat them as "black boxes" that store information in the form of records, and can be accessed from a program. By using the statements such as OPEN-, KILL-, PRINT#, READ#, IF END# .... THEN, and END (described on the following pages) in a program, you can PRINT and READ information on files.*

Both of these descriptions were written for non-DP users. But whereas the first example has an impersonal, passive construction, the second communicates with the reader directly and personally, simplifying data processing as much as possible.

*A Guide to Time Shared Basic. Cupertino, CA: Hewlett-Packard.

3. HAVE A PURPOSE

PURPOSE IS ESSENTIAL TO GOOD WRITING

If you want your reports, proposals, systems or programs documentation to be effective, you must have a purpose. It's purpose, or if you will theme, that holds together a piece of writing and gives it substance.

Take the user's guide as an example. Its subject may be a new text-editing system, an on-line information retrieval system, or a key-to-disk data entry system. But its sole purpose is to teach the user to be proficient with a certain system or procedure. Furthermore, the single purpose of a proposal is to win a contract. And the purpose of a feasibility study is to report whether a proposed project is economically and/or technically feasible, and to present possible alternatives to problem(s).

4. USE DIRECT, UNCOMPLICATED LANGUAGE

Some people blame the "computer illiterature" on DP professionals who want to impress readers with their technical expertise. Other people trace it back to the early days of the computer industry when any kind of documentation was acceptable. It would be nice to be able to agree with the second group. The fact is, however, that you can still find an alarmingly large number of rambling, obscure technical documents at most DP facilities. Here's an example:

CASE IN POINT

The PERFORM verb provides all linkage to and from procedures (subroutines). The paragraphs and/or sections named in the PERFORM statement will be executed once, or the number of times specified by integer, or as many times as necessary until the test condition is satisfied. If test-condition is true when the statement is encountered, the next sentence will be immediately executed.

Compare it with this description:

The PERFORM verb is one of the most powerful in the COBOL repertoire. What we are saying in this statement is that we want to carry out the instructions in another part of the program. They may be carried out just once, or a specified number of times or, as in this case, repeatedly until a certain condition is true.*

The latter is a good example of vigorous, informative, yet informal writing that is easy to understand and easy to follow.

5. GET TO THE POINT

If your audience wants to read lengthy, intricate sentences, they will read William Faulkner or James Joyce. Technical writing is not a showcase for complicated sentence structure, or flights of fancy. You will lose your audience if your sentences are so long that people must reread them, because they have forgotten what you said at the start. Consider this:

CASE IN POINT

To control another company, such ownership is not required; if another company is able to formulate, determine or veto basic business policy decisions of the offeror, such other company is considered to control, hence be the parent company of the offeror.

This piece of writing is quoted directly from a government Request For Proposal (RFP) for a computer-based management information system. There's nothing quite so frustrating as having to read text that meanders over mountains, through valleys, and across deserts before it gets to the point (if at all). If you are a politician, such writing may be an asset, but that's practically the only profession where ambiguity and pompousness is not only tolerated but cultivated. For example:

The continuing study of information needs and information-seeking behavior is seen as a necessary component of the project in order to make certain that the developing system is an adaptive system that is continually responsive to real information needs.

*Daniel D. McCracken, *A Simplified Guide to Structured COBOL Programming*. New York: Wiley, 1976.

Compare it with:

To develop a system that is truly responsive to the information requirements of the users, it is necessary to continue studying the users and the information they really need.

The edited version speaks for itself as a communication that is direct and to the point.

6. BE CONCISE BUT INFORMATIVE

If you write concisely about any subject, you describe it in the fewest possible words, but without sacrificing information, clarity, or interest.

DON'T MISTAKE BREVITY FOR CONCISENESS

Brevity is often mistaken for conciseness. And the resulting disconnected writing confuses and frustrates every one, except perhaps its originator. Here are some random examples from computer manuals:

"Key in client ID number not known"

"To date, key systems designed several modules"

"If error on Error Listing unresolved, see Error Listings"

7. USE PERSONAL NOT IMPERSONAL VIEWPOINT

There's nothing as lethal as long, boring passages written in impersonal style. If you're product oriented instead of people oriented, don't be surprised if your audience responds with a yawn. Conversely, if you communicate with your readers on a one-to-one basis, it's almost impossible to write rambling, pompous sentences.

Try to follow and understand at first reading these passages taken from government documents.

EXAMPLE

An initially unacceptable technical proposal which appears to be reasonably susceptible to being made acceptable may be discussed with the offeror and, if sufficiently clarified, then deemed acceptable.

Watch Out for Acronyms and Initials

ANOTHER EXAMPLE

In unusual circumstances, a specific request for an original document may be made; if such original documentation is not made available as requested, the contractor agrees to provide transportation and subsistence, at no cost to the State or the contract revenue, for the State's fiscal representatives to carry out their audit function at the principal offices of the contractor or other location of such records.

However, the government and large corporations don't have a monopoly on pretentious writing. Here's an example from a data processing manual for beginners:

STILL ANOTHER EXAMPLE

A flowchart is a graphic presentation of operations, data, flow, equipment, and procedures by which data are processed by programs accessing files in a computer based system which can be based in a large, medium, or mini computer. In a program flowchart the emphasis is on the operations and decisions necessary to complete the process.

Compare it with:

A flowchart is an outline, used to help write computer programs. Drawing a flowchart is a good way to express on paper the types and sequence of operations necessary to solve a problem. Flowcharts, however, are not an end but rather a means to the end of finding solutions to the problems.*

The writer of the last example is obviously people oriented. He communicates with his target audience—the beginning programmer—in a friendly but not condescending tone. Moreover, besides defining in simple terms the particular DP method, he mentions its limitation as well.

USE AS FEW ACRONYMS AND INITIALS AS POSSIBLE

8. WATCH OUT FOR ACRONYMS AND INITIALS

The data processing field is perhaps the worst offender in using acronyms and initials indiscriminately. Of course, government agencies are not far behind.

If you want to have some fun, ask a group of systems designers/analysts or programmers to define such commonly used acronyms as:

*A Guide to HP Educational Basic. Cupertino, CA: Hewlett-Packard, 1970.

LIST OF ACRONYMS

COBOL	Common Business-Oriented Language
BASIC	Beginners All-purpose Symbolic Instruction Code language
JCL	Job Control Language
RPG	Report Program Generator
TSO	Time-Sharing Option
HASP	Houston Automatic Spooling Program
BSAM	Basic Sequential Access Method
BDAM	Basic Direct Access Method
DD	Data Definition, or Data Dictionary

If they can describe half of these, they are above the norm for data processing personnel. Yet the majority of DP professionals expect the users, who are more often than not non-DP people, to understand computer jargon. You will increase your reader's understanding if you define the acronyms and initials the first time you use them. And in addition, just to be sure, list even the simplest acronyms in a glossary.

EDIT TO CUT OUT ALL THE FAT

9. EDIT TO ELIMINATE COMPLEXITY AND REDUNDANCY

Editing is an essential part of writing if you wish to produce useful document(s). When you edit, look for ways to cut and compress. Challenge every sentence to ensure that it gives valid information in the fewest possible simple words. Strike out superfluous adjectives, adverbs, articles, prepositions, and relative pronouns. For example, in the sentence "The programmer left out some OF THE subroutines assigned to him," or "The program listing THAT you gave me was delivered to the project leader," the words in capital letters should be eliminated for economy and easy reading. Simply put, check your sentences and delete all superfluous words.

In addition to editing out unnecessary words and phrases, check that you vary short sentences with longer ones and short paragraphs with longer ones. Moreover, see to it that the transitions from one paragraph to another, and from one concept to another are smooth. And finally, check that the document as a whole reflects its purpose.

Edit to Eliminate Complexity and Redundancy

The following three paragraphs are taken from the original version of a report on efforts to improve data entry resources at a commercial DP facility.

CASE IN POINT Formerly, the Company employed the usual keypunching procedure, where each clerk keypunched incoming data as rapidly as possible. The inevitable errors were corrected during verification, essentially a duplicate keypunching procedure. It was the wastefulness of that second keying that always bothered the data entry manager, because almost 90 percent of the Company's DP costs were related to data entry.

Also, formerly a clerk checked transaction forms as they came from the mailroom. Obvious errors were caught and corrected before the transaction forms went to the data entry stations. But even with the extra checking step, the Company was plagued with a large number of bad transactions that showed up during batch processing. One transaction in five was returned and had to be corrected manually and reentered—a costly and time-consuming process.

After studying the situation, the data entry manager came up with a more efficient method. Now, under the new time-and-cost-saving procedure devised by the data entry manager, the forms go directly from the mailroom to the data entry clerks. Only transactions that they can't correct on the fly are given to the "error" clerk. The results are significantly less number of bad transactions and reduced data entry costs, both of which please the data entry manager, not to mention the management.

Here's the drastically edited version of the same report:

For years the Company's DP data entry operations was a costly and time-consuming process. Though each transaction was keyed and verified, one transaction in five had to be returned and corrected manually to be reentered.

To make this procedure more efficient and economical, the data entry manager decided to have the forms go directly from the mailroom to the data entry clerks. Only transactions that are grossly incorrect are routed from the data entry staff to the "error" clerk. The results are significantly fewer bad transactions in batch processing and reduced costs, both of which please the data entry manager, not to mention the management.

Chapter Three
Defining Your Target Readers

A document may contain accurate data and sound logic, and be well organized, but unless it's written for a specific audience, its effectiveness is diffused. In addition, if it's product-oriented instead of reader-oriented, very few people will read or use that document. The tons of manuals, reports, and other communications gathering dust on the shelves of DP and DP-related organizations are tangible proofs of this waste of the DP professionals' time and effort in writing those documents, not to mention the cost to the company.

To ensure effective communication, first you define your audience and then you orient your material to them. Further, it's vital that the DP communicator understands that there are no "primary" and "secondary" audiences. All persons, whether their background is highly technical, semitechnical, or nontechnical, ARE primary audiences. And the DP professional preparing a communication should think in terms of satisfying the needs and preferences of each set of readers. That is, if the resulting document is to meet their approval.

Defining Your Target Readers

CONSIDER THE READER FIRST

1. READER-ORIENTED VERSUS PRODUCT-ORIENTED COMMUNICATIONS

Unfortunately, ever since its inception the DP industry has been concentrating on the product and more or less ignoring the customer. Only in the last few years have the customer's needs and preferences been systematically considered. Even now, however, too many technical communications, such as systems documentation, user's guides, operations manuals, and feasibility studies, give only superficial attention to the reader's requirements.

The same disregard for audiences can be seen in most of the independent seminars and workshops on "Technical Writing Skills." While they hammer away at the importance of written communications, and of maintaining clarity and brevity in presentations, few discuss the significance of the specific audience for whom the mountain of paperwork is being produced. Thus many independent courses actually propagate the concept of product-oriented communications.

It's noteworthy that readers at all levels of business organizations are expressing their dissatisfaction with DP documentation and reports, both within their organizations and in certain DP publications. Yet the industry, and more specifically many technical writers and systems analyst who write reports, proposals, and systems documentation, seem oblivious to these valid complaints. In any event, their written communications give no evidence of awareness of the criticism.

Theodore Levitt puts the whole thing into proper perspective by calling it "Marketing Myopia" and defining it thus:

PRODUCTS ARE SECONDARY

The view that an industry is a customer-satisfying process, not a goods-producing process, is vital for all businessmen to understand. An industry begins with the customer and his needs, not with a patent, a raw material, or a selling skill. Given the customer's needs, the industry develops backwards, first concerning itself with the physical delivery of *customer satisfaction*. Then it moves back further to creating the things by which these satisfactions are in part achieved. How these materials are created is a matter of indifference to the customer, hence the particular form of manufacturing, processing, or what have you, cannot be considered as a vital aspect of the industry.*

THE RIGHT DOCUMENT TO THE RIGHT PEOPLE

The technical communicator who is preoccupied with the product (hardware, software, application, procedures, or standards), and pays little or no attention to his or her readers and their requirements, produces useless material. To avoid this pitfall, as soon as you have a general idea of the proposed subject, begin your project by studying the prospective readers. Once you define your audience and zero in on their basic needs and preferences, take a closer look at your product and find out how its readers will use it. Next, determine the style, vocabulary, and format of the document according to its readers and intended usage. When all this is done, only then you study the product IN DEPTH.

2. WHO IS YOUR TARGET AUDIENCE?

Because there are many levels of communication in data processing, it's necessary to define your target audience. Audiences have different needs and different preferences. And the same subject has to be presented on a different level for each particular target audience. For example, highly technical DP documentation usually is beyond the grasp and need of non-DP readers; thus such writing is useless to them. Conversely, simplified non-technical material tends to be boring to highly technical DP readers; thus such a document is worthless to them. In short, well-written material given to the wrong people is just as useless as badly written material. In either case you have toiled in vain, because your document is neither going to be read nor used. That's why it's essential to define your communications in line with what you perceive to be your audience and their needs.

*"Marketing Myopia," by Theodore Levitt, in *Modern Marketing Strategy*, edited by Edward C. Bursk and John F. Chapman. Cambridge, MA: Harvard University Press, 1964.

3. AIM AT YOUR READER'S INTEREST LEVEL

Take the DP audience, for example. Even within a particular computer facility there are many levels of data processing competence and interest. Here again, to provide the right information to each user, you have to start by defining your target audience. The DP staff under a hierarchy of management may include:

GIVE THE USER THE RIGHT AMOUNT OF INFORMATION AT THE RIGHT LEVEL

a. **Systems analysts/designers,** who use the computer services at both system and user levels. They require a high degree of technical completeness in systems documentation, systems studies, and reports.

b. **Systems programmers**, who use most computer services. Because of their diverse responsibilities, they also require a high degree of technical completeness in systems, operations, programs documentation, and software descriptions.

c. **Applications and maintenance programmers**, who use some system and many user-level functions of the computer services. They require direct and concise technical language in documentation and communications. These programmers, however, do not need or want the in-depth treatment that systems programmers require.

d. **Technical applications users**, such as quality control staff or computer operators, who use a fixed set of functions to do one or more tasks repeatedly. They need clear and succinct technical language in the documentation of a particular set of functions.

e. **Nontechnical applications users**, such as word processing, data entry, or data preparation clerks, who use a small, fixed set of user functions to do one or more tasks repeatedly. They require easy to understand instructions written in nontechnical language.

f. **Professional nontechnical applications users**, such as auditors, controllers, accountants, cost analysts, and the like, who use a definitive set of user functions. They require nontechnical but more sophisticated language than the previous category of users.

Aim at Your Reader's Interest Level

YOU DON'T NEED A SEPARATE MANUAL FOR EACH CATEGORY

Defining the target audience, however, does not mean writing a separate manual for each of the above categories. That would be a horrendous task, and anyway the categories are not totally isolated from each other.

The systems analysts, systems programmers, and applications/maintenance programmers fall into one group, and their requirements can be satisfied with a SYSTEM AND PROGRAMMING MANUAL. (In case of a large and complicated system, however, the manual should be in two volumes to avoid a massive and awkward book.)

A RUNBOOK or OPERATIONS MANUAL can meet the needs of the computer operators.

CAUTION

Don't make the mistake, however, of trying to cut down on your work load by lifting the program documentation from the System and Programming Manual and giving it to the computer operators. It will not satisfy their requirements because these technicians RUN JOBS (each job may contain one or more programs) and NOT PROGRAMS. What computer operators need and want is a runbook for each application (or system or subsystem) such as accounts receivable, accounts payable, pricing subsystem, and company pension system.

TAILOR YOUR USER'S GUIDE TO THE AUDIENCE

The nontechnical and professional nontechnical applications users' requirements can be met with a USER'S GUIDE. Of course, you would not write a user's guide describing, for example, an inquiry/retrieval system for clerks in field offices in the same language and style as for scientists or executives. Though both of these audiences are non-DP people, the vocabulary, approach, and format would have to be different to meet their specific requirements and level of needed information. This doesn't mean, however, that the clerks' manual is written in "Dick and Jane" prose, nor that the manual for the professional readers is written in "educated" prose. It just means toning your material to reach your different readers.

NOTE: Remember that systems analysts, systems programmers, and applications programmers, having a sound knowledge of data processing, require the greatest amount of detail and conciseness of data in their documents. Nontechnical users, on the other hand, having a limited knowledge of data processing, require extreme clarity in explanations, and simplicity in instructions. For example, a part of the INPUT-PROCESSING paragraph of the logic narrative for a credit-checking program used by the DP staff might give the following information:

EXAMPLE

The INPUT-PROCESSING section reads three different types of Customer Files. A Customer Extract File is read first for the purpose of building an Internal Table. This file has the same data elements as the Master File. Since the Extract File is actually a truncated Customer Record, it is necessary to select the needed data elements.

Compare this with the instructions given to nontechnical applications users in a user's guide:

There are five simple steps to read customers' records:

1. Sign on to the network.
2. Enter your command to get the Customer Record File.
3. Enter the specific information you want to see.
4. Read the particular customer record.
5. Sign off the network.

PROPOSALS

Another occasion when it's crucial to define your readers is when writing a proposal. Normally, a proposal is divided into three parts, each part being a distinct entity directed to a different audience. These three parts are:

WRITE MANAGEMENT OVERVIEW IN NEAR-MARKETING STYLE

PART I, the Management Overview, which presents the proposed system in an easy-to-read, narrative form. To capture and hold the attention of the contract administrator or "first reader," who usually is a non-DP person, it should be free of DP jargon, unencumbered by technical details, and written in a near-marketing style. Customarily, the first reader determines whether the pro-

Writing To and Not For Management

posal complies in general with the Request For Proposal (RFP), Request For Quotation (RFQ), or (division/department) service request. Subsequently, the proposal is sent with the first reader's comments to management, who usually are also non-DP people. This procedure applies to both vendor and in-house proposals at most commercial and government facilities.

WRITE TECHNICAL DISCUSSION IN CLEAR, CONCISE TECHNICAL LANGUAGE

PART II, the Technical Discussion, which is read and studied by technical people who tend to dislike marketing style writing. Consequently, you should use technical language. Moreover, include as many details of the proposed system as can be provided at this juncture.

WRITE PRICE QUOTATIONS IN TERSE, NONTECHNICAL LANGUAGE

PART III, the Cost/Pricing Analysis, which is usually examined painstakingly by the customer's accounting department, specifically, by the controller. This audience is again different from the readers of the two previous parts. Controllers and other finance-oriented people generally dislike both the marketing and the highly technical type of writing. Consequently, you can reach them by giving them an unembroidered statement of what tangible benefits can be expected from the system; the expertise of the staff who will work on the project; and the cost and estimated schedule of each phase of the system based on the data given to you by your company's cost analyst and systems designer.

DON'T OVER- OR UNDERESTIMATE MANAGEMENT

4. WRITING TO AND NOT FOR MANAGEMENT

Many DP Professionals freeze when they are asked to write a report or some other form of communication to management. Their writing becomes stiff, pretentious, and boring. If the same people would stop trying to impress management, stop trying to dazzle management by being "clever," and just relax and communicate the needed information directly and simply, the resulting document would have the desired effect.

When writing to management, you should assume that you're addressing an intelligent audience. And to reach these people, to make them receptive to your ideas or viewpoint, or your particular way of presenting a subject, don't clutter your communication with details. Management has neither the time nor the inclination to absorb details. As decision makers, their responsibility is to make decisions based on the "big picture" with only enough details to delineate the tip of the iceberg. Then they delegate the study and analysis of the project to personnel on a lower level.

In a communication to management, the material itself should be structured clearly and organized logically. It should begin at the beginning, progress in a straight line, and end at the ending, without jumping back and forth between topics. Otherwise, management might lose interest in the information you're trying to relay, and thus might lose interest in you.

DON'T WASTE YOUR PEERS' TIME

5. WRITING TO PEERS

When communicating to your peers, whether it's through documentation, memo, or on-line CRT (cathode ray tube) terminal, you should be direct and informative, yet be brief and to the point. No one, and that includes your peers, likes to waste valuable time on verbose, confusing communications.

If you're one of the many people who cannot discuss an event, subject, or idea concisely, try this: write an outline of your material first. When the skeleton is completed, it's relatively easy to put "meat" on the "bare bones" and produce a piece of writing that you can be satisfied with, if not proud of. Don't forget, however, that once you sign and send out a written communication—even one directed to your peers—you can never be sure on whose desk it will end up.

6. WRITING TO SUBORDINATES

TODAY'S SUBORDINATES MAY BE TOMORROW'S SUPERIORS

Your communications to subordinates should never have a patronizing tone. If you have a condescending attitude toward your subordinates, it will show in your written communications, no matter how carefully you try to hide it. A person in a subordinate position is not necessarily less intelligent or less competent than you are. Remember: today's subordinate may be tomorrow's peer and next week's supervisor, or even manager.

7. WRITING TO THE PUBLIC

DIFFERENT DP PUBLICATIONS CATER TO DIFFERENT AUDIENCES

The analysis and definition of the target audience is essential when the DP professional is writing to the public. Within the DP technical publications there is a vast difference in style, format, and subject. For example, writing an article for COMMUNICATIONS OF THE ACM (Association for Computing Machinery) is quite different than writing an article for DATAMATION, COMPUTERWORLD, COMPUTER DECISIONS, INPUT, or INFOSYSTEMS. There may be similarity in concepts, but the audiences are worlds apart.

Discounting the esoteric and sometimes pedantic articles that, it seems, are written solely by university and college professors and published by various professional and scientific association magazines, articles for commercial publications must follow a few rules. That is, if they are to be accepted for publication and paid for. These rules are:

1. The article should address a topic or problem the particular audience is concerned with.
2. The lead paragraph must be simple and direct. It should summarize the article, and it should not mislead the reader.
3. The material should hold the readers' attention until the very last word. And it will, if you observe the previously discussed mechanics of good writing.

Chapter Four
Steps Prior to Writing

When starting on a project that involves written communications between you and management, you and the end user, or you and the systems staff, or programmers, or computer operators (DP technicians, if you will), certain preliminary steps are necessary to ensure a meaningful and useful finished copy.

The range and depth of research and other preparation steps you do PRIOR to writing will determine the quality and effectiveness of your completed work. Correspondingly, most meaningless, disorganized documents are the result of careless, superficial preparation. Therefore, as soon as your project is approved and the assignment given to you, make up a formal plan to accomplish your project.

NOTE: Proper planning is as essential for producing effective written communications as is for developing an efficient, economical computer system.

Although planning methods may vary from facility to facility, certain requirements such as comprehensive preparation, control, and completion of project on schedule are universal, and must be included in the planned steps prior to writing.

Here's one sequence of planned steps or approach for addressing and meeting these requirements.

1. **Define** the project.
2. **Gather** data.
3. **Get** the most out of interviews.
4. **Check** the software.
5. **Organize** the collected data.
6. **Determine** your document's personality.
7. **Outline** your material.

8. **Summarize** your subject.
9. **Define** the layout and content format standards.

(Of course, if your organization has established format standards, you should adhere to them.)

NOTE: Not all of these steps are applicable to every type of communication. You will have to select the ones that are appropriate to your particular document.

FACTORS TO CONSIDER WHEN UNDERTAKING A WRITING PROJECT

1. DEFINE THE PROJECT

a. **By defining and establishing the objective** of your project, you clarify the goal of your assignment and set the direction for your efforts. If, for instance, you have defined that the objective of your communication will be to relay to management whether QA (quality assurance) is effectively enforced in the company's DP facility, you would examine and write about QA's role. Specifically, you would describe how QA monitors the flow of work; how it functions to maintain established standards of manual and computer operations; how it alerts operators when the standards are not adhered to; and how well or poorly performance and resource management criteria are met.

b. **By setting up the scope** or the extent, if you will, of the writing project, you can realistically estimate how much information you will need to collect and present in your communication. If, for instance, the scope of your progress report covers events, performance, and problems of the last three months only, you will not need to gather data for the whole year. You may, however, wish to make a brief general statement alluding to the prior period.

c. **By defining the audience* and the usage** of your proposed document, you are able to determine the level of information, the style and language you will use. These

---
*Details on defining the audience were discussed in the preceding chapter.

Gather Data

factors, in turn, will affect the personality of your finished product. (See section 6 of this chapter.)

d. By establishing a tentative schedule, you can determine the approximate number of hours or days you can spend on each phase of your document to ensure that it will be finished on target.

HOW TO COLLECT INFORMATION

2. GATHER DATA

When you collect information in a systematic way, you not only acquire the data necessary for your communication, you also become familiar with the organization, its manual and computer operations, and its people. Depending on the type and level of document you will write, you can use several approaches to collect information. Two of the better known methods are called "top-down" and "bottom-up." (Obviously, the terminology is borrowed from Structured Programming Technique.)

a. The "top-down" approach consists of:

- **Getting an overview** from organization charts to learn how the enterprise/division/department is structured. (You may not use the organization charts in your document, if, for example, you are documenting an application system, but knowing the "big picture" will help you to figure out who's reporting to whom. This bit of information can be valuable later when your document is ready for approval, or when you need a response to a particular communication.)
- **Reading office correspondence** to determine the level of communication within the company (if it's an in-house project), or with the customer (if it's an external project). Existing communications have a great bearing on the tone, style, and depth of detail of your own material.
- **Examining existing corporate policy and procedure manuals** as well as the documentation standards, if you are a new hire or if you work on a contract and are not familiar with the firm's policies, procedures, and standards.

- **Reviewing job descriptions** to determine the responsibilities and tasks involved in certain jobs such as data control, computer/console operations, data entry, and similar tasks. Such information is essential when writing procedures for clerical or computer operations staff.

NOTE: In addition, you should, if at all possible, observe firsthand how such jobs are performed. Sometimes job descriptions are not complete or accurate.

RESEARCH, INTERVIEWS, AND FIRSTHAND OBSERVATIONS ARE ESSENTIAL

- **Finding out the requirements** of the user/customer by interviewing the DP staff as well as the non-DP employees, if your document will be used by non-DP people. For example, if you are writing a user manual for an existing data entry system, you would interview both the systems analyst and/or programmer who designed and programmed that system, AND the data entry staff. The latter may have limited knowledge of computer technology, but they have been trained to operate that system. Interviews with the data entry operators will ensure that your document will be meaningful to current employees and useful to new hires.

b. The **"bottom-up"** approach consists of the same steps as the "top-down" approach, only in reverse order. Specifically, you start interviewing the front line employees and work up to the supervisor and manager, and only then do you review the organization charts.

If you get the impression that interviewing is crucial in gathering data and information, you are quite right. And for that reason a discussion on effective interviewing techniques follow.

PREPARE FOR YOUR INTERVIEWS

3. GET THE MOST OUT OF INTERVIEWS

Interviews that are carefully prepared, skillfully conducted, and tightly controlled will provide the most information for the least effort. Conversely, without proper preparation much valuable time can be wasted, yours as well as that of the interviewee.

a. **Securing appointments** with the interviewees is an essential step in your preparation. That, however, can be quite frustrating in certain situations. A good way of overcoming the "I'm too busy now" syndrome is to schedule the making of the appointment at least one or two days in advance.

A NOTE OF CAUTION: Unless the person you need to interview sits at the very next desk, generally it's better to make an appointment for the interview by telephone. For some unfathomable reason, no matter how busy a person is, if you get him or her on the telephone, he/she will try to squeeze your interview into his/her schedule. But if you approach the same individual face to face, you may be waved off with "Not now. Try me in another month or so."

CONSIDER THE INTERVIEWEE'S SCHEDULE

b. **Showing consideration** of the person's schedule is very important. Tell him or her, as you request an appointment, approximately how long the interview will take. Everyone's time is valuable, and you are more likely to get an interview with a busy person if you establish a timetable for the event. But establishing a timetable is not enough. You have to follow it through. And that means being thoroughly prepared for the interview by compiling a list of questions and the results you expect from the interview, keeping in mind the objective of your future document. Of course, the questions should be based on the in-depth research you have already conducted.

c. **Listening attentively** once you are into the meeting, except for asking the prepared questions, is a key factor in successful interviews. To get valid and quality information, word your questions so as to give the interviewee an opportunity to demonstrate his or her knowledge, and let him or her know that you value and respect this expertise. Moreover, you have to be flexible. Often, despite comprehensive preparation, you will have to follow up the interviewee's answers with questions that you have not prepared. For example, if the interviewee happens to mention that a new product is scheduled to be installed in the DP facility, or that a certain procedure (related to your assignment) is going to be changed in the near future, you should ask for further details. Such information is vital to the timeliness of your document.

CRITICAL POINT: YOU CONTROL THE MEETING, NOT THE INTERVIEWEE

d. **You must be in control** of the interview from beginning to end. You ask the questions; you bring the conversation back to points that need clarification; you guide the flow of discussion; and you terminate the interview. Of course, you do all this unobtrusively and gently but firmly.

TAPE-RECORD THE INTERVIEW, IF POSSIBLE

e. **It's best to tape-record the meeting,** since note taking is not only inefficient but may also inhibit the interviewee. Of course, you ask the interviewee's permission to tape his or her responses at the time you make the appointment. But when you explain that with this medium there's no chance of misunderstanding his or her words, or leaving out any important statement, most people will agree to have the interview taped. In fact, even those who are reluctant to permit it usually give their consent if you promise to submit to them the final, typed copy BEFORE it is sent out, or submitted to top management, or used in a manual.

KEEP YOUR OPINIONS TO YOURSELF

f. **During an interview** *never* **give your opinion** on any policy, system, or procedure the company is using; *never* show bias about any person within the organization; and *never* relay to the interviewee anything that you heard from a previously interviewed person. The reason for keeping your opinion and thoughts to yourself is that the interviewee might repeat your words—colored with his or her own views—to other people. And before you know it, a casual remark by you becomes a big and perhaps embarrassing issue. The same thing applies for repeating comments from another interviewee.

Get the Most Out of Interviews

TRANSCRIBE THE TAPE OR NOTES

g. **If you tape the interview, have it transcribed** as soon as possible. If you take notes, it's very important right after the interview to expand your notes while the information is fresh in your mind. Then, have the notes typed, or type them yourself at the earliest opportunity.

COMPARE TRANSCRIPT WITH LIST OF QUESTIONS

h. **Finally, compare the content** of your typed transcript with your listed questions as well as your previously defined objectives. If a topic or detail was left out of the interview, don't feel embarrassed or shy about calling up the interviewee and asking for additional information. If you have done your job and established rapport, the person will agree to answer a few more questions.

In sum, the ground rules for an effective interview are:

- Do comprehensive research. The more sophisticated or complex the computer system you have to document, or propose (if it's a proposal), or evaluate (if it's a feasibility study), the more detailed your research should be before you start interviewing people.
- Write a carefully thought-out list of questions, and the expected results.
- Control the interview.
- Establish a good relationship with the interviewee.
- Review the written interview against your initial list.

NOTE: As stated before, the decision as to whom to choose to be interviewed depends on the nature of your assignment. For example, if you are writing a computer operations manual/runbook, you would interview the supervisor/lead computer operator and one or two subordinates he or she recommends. But before you even make an appointment with the supervisor, it's essential that you interview the manager. This accomplishes two things:

1. Getting management overview of the computer operations, and
2. Winning the manager's support for your future document.

CHECK THE SYSTEM YOURSELF

4. CHECK THE SOFTWARE BY USING IT

When documenting a computer system or application, or preparing a user's guide for a software package, you must use the system. This is to ensure that your document will be accurate, even if the information from the interviewee(s) happens to be inaccurate. In other words, verify that the system works as the interviewee(s) said it does.

ORGANIZE YOUR DATA TO ACHIEVE YOUR PROJECT'S OBJECTIVE

5. ORGANIZE THE COLLECTED DATA

The objective of your assignment dictates the sequence or priorities (by order, time, or importance) of how the data will be organized.

If, for example, the objective of your document is to acquaint the DP staff with a new software package and its usage, you wouldn't feature on the very first page a compiled, tested program, presuming that most of the DP professionals are acquainted with it.

To be on the safe side, you would assume that the DP staff has no knowledge of the new package. Consequently, you would use the *hierarchical order* of presentation. You would lead the reader from a briefly stated objective and a method of using and updating the manual, through a description of the package's features, and to detailed procedures for using these features. Only then would you present a compiled and tested program. (Example follows.) Hierarchical order of presentation would also be appropriate for systems documentation.

If the objective of your document is to instruct mailroom or data control clerks, data entry operators, or computer operators about a certain procedure, you would organize and present your material in *chronological sequence.* You would start at the beginning of the procedure and proceed step-by-step to the end of the procedure. (Example follows.)

If the objective of your manual is to inform students about the capabilities and services of their school's com-

Organize the Collected Data

puter center, as well as how the current facilities evolved, you would employ the *spatial or place order* of presentation, focusing on how and where. (Example follows.)

If the objective of your document is to provide a feasibility study that examines, evaluates, and perhaps recommends a certain system to solve a particular problem of the company, you would organize your data to respond to three main questions in order of *increasing importance*. These are:

- Is the proposed system economically feasible?
- Is it operationally feasible?
- Is it technically feasible?

On the other hand, if you are writing a solicited, formal proposal, the organization of the material by necessity would follow the structure and format as stated in the RFP (Request For Proposal) or RFQ (Request For Quotation). Even if you are writing an unsolicited proposal or an informal proposal responding to an in-house service request, your data should be organized according to the generally accepted proposal structure and format. (Proposals are detailed in Part III.)

SAMPLE **Hierarchical Order Presentation**

BASE TIME-SHARING SYSTEM
USER'S GUIDE

I. INTRODUCTION

The purpose of this manual is to aid both new and experienced time-sharing users in the efficient and effective use of the Base Time-Sharing System (B T/SS). To achieve this objective and provide you the basic information to define, develop, and implement B T/SS applications, this User's Guide includes:

- An overview of B T/SS facilities and capabilities.
- Step-by-step procedures for getting ON and OFF the system; using the user-oriented command language; using the Base Editor for creating/modifying files; and using other vital features of the B T/SS.
- Detailed information on the services is available to B T/SS users from the in-house B T/SS Support Group.

A. Using and Updating the Manual

For ease of reference, the manual is divided into 10 sections. Each section delineates a few related components of B T/SS, and is marked with an appropriate tab. To keep the manual current, updates, corrections, and additions will be distributed to all B T/SS users. The updates are to be inserted into the User's Guide, and the obsolete pages removed and thrown away.

SAMPLE Time-Order Presentation

MAILROOM PROCEDURES

Task	Action
Process and distribute mail that consists of checks, address changes, and correspondence. Control forms used in this processing: Request Letter #10–10. Transmittal Entry Form #10–04.	Each morning receive mail. Open envelopes and extract contents. Sort mail into three groups: 1. Checks. 2. Address changes. 3. Correspondence. Place the last two items in their appropriate distribution boxes. Next, sort the check items into two groups: 1. Checks without coupons. 2. Checks with coupons. Look for the client's account number on checks *without coupons*. If there are any checks without coupons and *no account numbers*, return them to the clients with a request letter and a self-addressed stamped envelope (SASE). Verify that checks—both with and without coupons—have been endorsed. If there are any checks with no signature, return them to the clients with a request letter and a SASE. Finally, route all verified checks and coupons with a transmittal entry form to the encoding operator in the encoding room.

SAMPLE **Spatial or Place Order Presentation**

STENTON COLLEGE DATA
PROCESSING FACILITY
USER'S MANUAL

I. INTRODUCTION

A. History

The installation of an IBM Card Programmed Calculator in the basement of Starr Hall in March 1953 marked the establishment of Stenton College's Data Processing Center. As computing grew at Stenton, so did the role of the DP Center. And now it includes all major computing activities at the college. To better service this growing and sophisticated user community, the center has been reorganized into several facilities. The computers located in Starr Hall became the Campus Facility; the ARIN Facility, part of Artificial Intelligence Laboratory, was formed to provide the special computation requirements associated with the laboratory; and the MED Facility, a research project sponsored by the National Institutes of Health for the purpose of furthering medical research, was created to handle the needs of this project.

B. Organization

Although each facility is physically separate from the other centers, the responsibility for coordination, control, and operation is vested in the DP Center as a whole. In this way, Stenton College's computer expertise is consolidated for the benefit of everyone. The following pages discuss in detail the hardware/software configurations, capabilities, and key personnel of each facility.

Outline your Material

TOTAL PICTURE OF DOCUMENT = PERSONALITY

6. DETERMINE YOUR DOCUMENT'S PERSONALITY

The "personality" of a manual, report, proposal, or marketing brochure is not one single thing. It's the words you use, the way you present the subject, the format, the paper, the color of the cover or binder, and even the type font you choose. A document will be rejected and all your efforts wasted, unless its personality satisfies its readers. Thus a user's guide, for example, should have a personality different from that of a systems documentation, or an interoffice memo. Simply put, if you tailor your communications to satisfy your audience's needs and preferences, your document's personality will reflect that effort. It also will be more meaningful and useful to its readers.

AN OUTLINE HELPS YOU ACHIEVE A STRUCTURED DOCUMENT

7. OUTLINE YOUR MATERIAL

Writing an outline of the proposed subject *before* you do any actual writing is important, because it can facilitate the writing of the most complex topics. It can also save you a lot of effort in producing the document, and serve as an effective control mechanism as well. Some people consider the outline—a schematic statement of the subject—an indispensable tool for producing useful documents. Moreover, if there are changes in the to-be-documented system, or manual or computer procedures *after* you have done your research and conducted your interviews (as it usually happens in most DP facilities), it will be easy to revise only the affected section(s) of your outline. And you can do this without deviating from the objective and scope of your document. In other words, by preparing an outline you are breaking down the project into modules or blocks of related information. This in turn enables you to move around the modules or information blocks to their most effective places in the written presentation.

There are several outline formats. Depending on the length and complexity of the project, you may choose the summary outline, the skeletal outline, or the detailed outline.

a. The summary outline is a sketchy schematic. It consists of the main headings only. For example:

Title: SALES OPERATIONS SYSTEM

USER MANUAL

CHAPTER I.	GENERAL SYSTEM OVERVIEW
CHAPTER II.	INPUT DESCRIPTION
CHAPTER III.	OUTPUT DESCRIPTION
CHAPTER IV.	PROCEDURES DESCRIPTION
CHAPTER V.	CLERICAL PROCEDURES
CHAPTER VI.	OPERATIONS PROCEDURES
	GLOSSARY

b. The skeletal outline is the most often used type of outline. Here the main headings of sections or modules are broken down into subsections. This segmentation enables you to work independently on any subsection without disturbing the total structure. For example:

Title: SALES OPERATIONS SYSTEM

USER MANUAL

CHAPTER I.   GENERAL SYSTEM OVERVIEW
CHAPTER II.   INPUT DESCRIPTION
                     A.   Line Item
                     B.   Scheduled Delivery
                     C.   Actual Delivery
CHAPTER III.   OUTPUT DESCRIPTION
                     A.   Device/Sales Status Report
                     B.   Summary of Shipments
                     C.   Period/Sales/Backlog Status Report
                     D.   Sales Operations Master File
                     E.   Exception Reports
CHAPTER IV.   PROCEDURES DESCRIPTION
                     A.   Change Order
                     B.   Blanket Order
                     C.   Lot Charges
                     D.   Input Forms

CHAPTER V.   CLERICAL PROCEDURES
  A. Special Keying Instructions
  B. Retention Periods
  C. Disposition of Inputs/Outputs
  D. Processing Schedule

CHAPTER VI. OPERATIONS PROCEDURES
  A. Job Flowcharts and Descriptions
  B. Operations Requirements
  C. System Error Messages
  D. Restart Procedures
  E. Daily Reports
  F. Weekly Reports

GLOSSARY

c. **The detailed outline** differs from the skeletal outline in that the subheadings are extended to a brief description of each subitem's contents. For example:

Title: SALES OPERATIONS SYSTEM

USER MANUAL

CHAPTER I.   GENERAL SYSTEM OVERVIEW
CHAPTER II.   INPUT DESCRIPTION
  A. **Line item record** is maintained by the Marketing Department from its copy of the sales orders. It contains data such as the device number, sales order number, item number, and job order number.
  B. **Scheduled delivery record** is maintained by Production Control. It gives the date and quantity the Production Department is committed to. There are multiple entries if partial shipments are scheduled.
  C. **Actual delivery record** is maintained by Production Control. It is a record of the actual shipment.

CHAPTER III. OUTPUT DESCRIPTION
  A. **The Device/Sales Status Report** is generated daily. It lists all open sales orders.

B. **The Summary of Shipments Report** is generated weekly. It summarizes the quantity and sales amount ordered, shipped, and backlogged for each open sales order line item.
C. **The Period/Sales/Backlog Status Report** is run on request from the Marketing Department, and is a summary of shipments for a given period of time.

A SUMMARY IS A SYNTHESIS OF YOUR MATERIAL

8. **SUMMARIZE YOUR SUBJECT**

By summarizing the content of your document, you will be forced to think through your assignment; to state your subject and objective clearly and concisely on one page. Moreover, you can use your summary as part of your introduction in the finished product. For example:

Title: SALES OPERATIONS SYSTEM

USER MANUAL

Summary

The Sales Operations System (SOS), a subsystem of the Management Information System (MIS), is designed to control the company's sales operations; to provide data for the Inventory Control System (ICS); and to give the Marketing Department timely information on sales. It is run daily to maintain an up-to-date Sales Operations Master File, and to generate daily and weekly reports.

STANDARDIZE THE LAYOUT AND CONTENT FORMATS

9. **DEFINE THE LAYOUT AND CONTENT FORMAT STANDARDS**

It's essential to define both the layout and the content formats of your document *before* the act of writing. If the organization can provide established format standards, all you have to do is follow them. However, if no standards exist, or if management indicates dissatisfac-

Define the Layout and Content Format Standards 51

tion with the current formats, then it's up to you to establish documentation standards.

While each facility should have tailor-made standards, all such material should include the following format standards.

a. **The layout format standards** define:

- The text format.
- The headings and subheadings.
- The numbering schemes.
- The particular paper to be used.
- The particulr typewriter font to be used.
- The type and number of tabs to be used.

- The text format specifies which type of document is to have double-spaced or two-column single-spaced format, and how wide the margins are to be around the text. For example, the systems documentation manuals are usually double-spaced, while operations manuals are often two-column single-spaced. User manuals can be in either format, depending on who the particular users are. The margins, however, should be generous regardless of the format used. This means 1 1/2 to 2 inches on top, 1 1/2 inch on the left, 3/4 inch on the right, and 1 inch on the bottom. These are just guidelines, and you set your own margins. The main thing is that once you establish the text format, that format is used consistently in all the manuals at your facility.
- The headings and subheadings standards state whether they will be all capital letters or only initial letters capital, and whether they will be underlined or not.
- The numbering schemes standards specify whether to use Roman numbers (I, II, III), or arabic numbers (1, 2, 3), or a combination of them, or even a combination of Roman and arabic numbers and the alphabet.
- The particular paper to be used is also defined. For example, in choosing paper, either 20-pound or 16-pound white paper would serve well.

- The particular typewriter font to be used is usually selected for ease of reading (even if a word-processing computer system is used). For example, the Courier 10 or dual Gothic 72 type font would fill this requirement.
- The type and number of tabs to be used is usually defined according to the type and width of the document. For example, a reference manual should have more tabs than an operations manual, and a document intended for heavy usage should have laminated tabs to survive all the handling.

Finally, the quality and color of binders as well as the size of the company logo (if there's one) for the internal documents must be determined. Of course, a two-page report doesn't need a binder, but manuals should be in three-ring, 1 or 2 or 2½ inch attractive vinyl binders.

b. The content format standards should state the criteria that must be met for each type of document such as systems documentation, programming manuals, runbooks, or user guides produced at the facility. Although the format selected will depend on the particular field in which the enterprise is operating, the target audience, and the type of material generated, all attractive formats share the following features:

Liberal use of headings and illustrations.

Wide margins (so that the text can "breathe").

Consistency in the numbering scheme.

Chapter Five
Mechanics of Data Processing Graphics

Graphics is an effective tool to pictorially express ideas, theories, facts, corporate structures, flow of systems, flow of operations, flow of manual work, and many other concepts. Moreover, graphics in DP written communications includes much more than just flowcharts, diagrams, and tables. Graphics, in fact, is central to documentation techniques such as HIPO (Hierarchy plus Input, Process, and Output) and SADT (Structure Analysis and Design Technique) for visual presentations of systems, procedures, and programs before, during, and after the design, development, and implementation stages.

Simply stated, graphics—whether drawn manually or via automated processing—is an easy means to explain technical topics to nontechnical people, because they can see, follow, and readily comprehend the visual description. Consequently, it's unfortunate that more people in the DP field don't use graphics to convey information to the user, especially since DP professionals normally employ graphics in every phase of systems development cycle. It is axiomatic that one page of graphics can replace many pages of conventional, sometimes tedious text and succeed in making the subject clear if not interesting.

Graphics used in the DP field consist of the following categories:

1. CHARTS

It's an interesting phenomenon that communicators both in and out of DP environments freely use organizational charts as a means of presenting the structure of an enterprise, division, or department. However, some of these same people will use text instead of charts to describe projects, information flow, and even extensive hardware configurations. Of the legion of charts, two types are most useful: flowcharts and diagrams.

a. Flowcharts. Data processing flowcharts are used at the conceptual, system overview, detail program, computer operations, and manual procedure levels. They serve to present: data flow, control flow, system, file, program, or record structures, as well as the steps necessary to complete a particular job or operation. Specifically, flowcharts display how systems, files, programs, computer processings, and manual procedures (related to data processing) work. They also show how the data and/or information flows through the enterprise and through specific systems.

NOTE: All flowcharts should be drawn using standard flowchart symbols (Figure 1).

The major flowchart types are:

FLOWCHARTS ARE EFFECTIVE VISUAL PRESENTATIONS OF ALMOST ANY KIND OF STRUCTURE OR ACTIVITY

- **Conceptual flowchart.** A pictorial presentation of the flow of information through all divisions and departments of the enterprise. The purpose of this flowchart is to show information flow paths through various divisions/departments. Consequently, it should be a stand-alone, self-explanatory graphics, to give management an accurate picture of the flow of information through the company. As the sample flowchart (Figure 2) shows, the division and departments are presented in horizontal layers, and the flow of information through the divisions or departments is vertical.

Charts

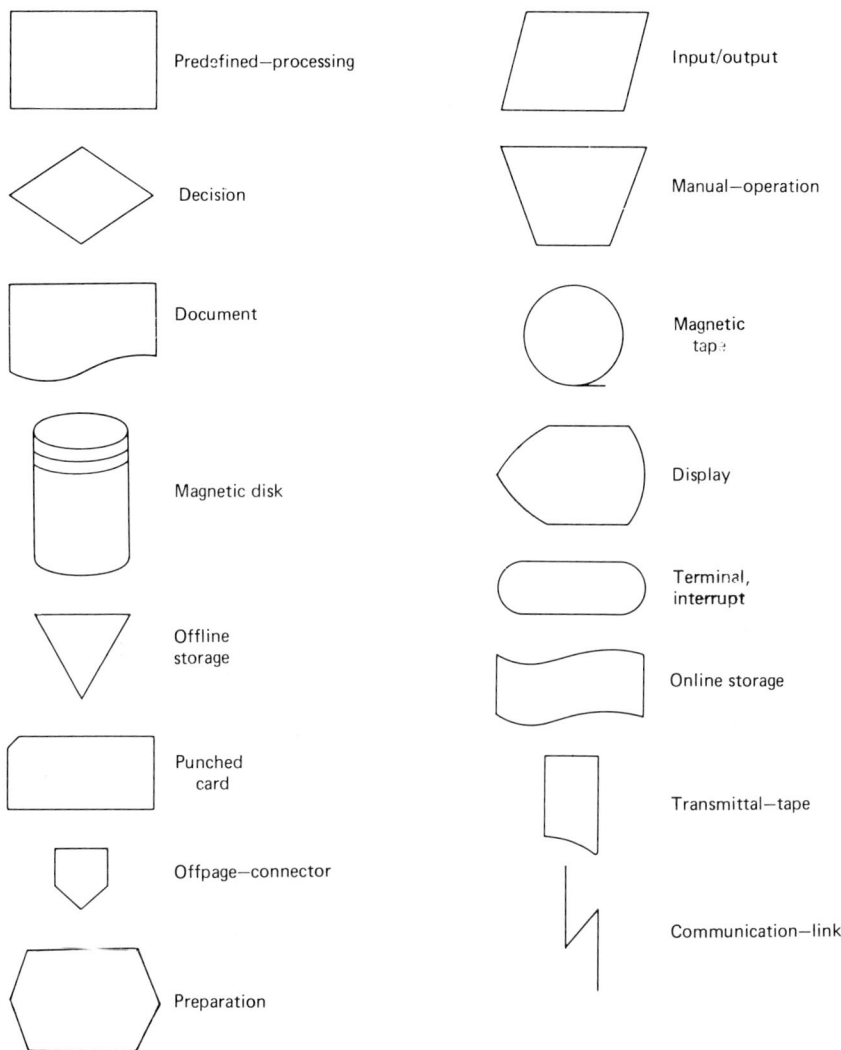

Figure 1. Standard flowchart symbols.

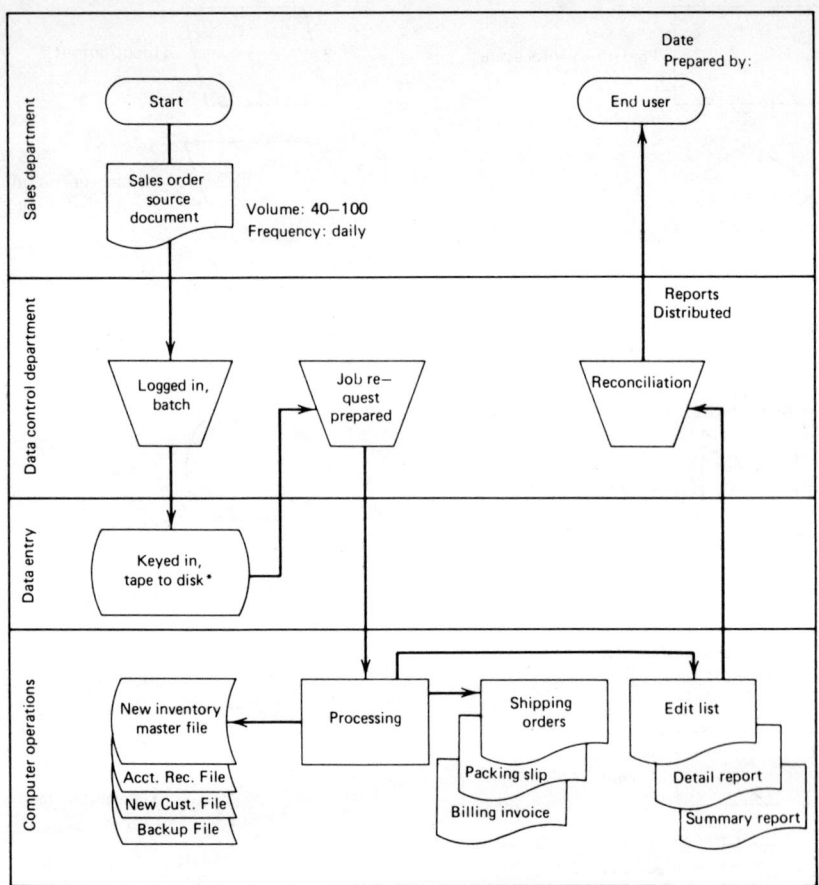

Figure 2. Sample: Sales inventory system conceptual flowchart.

- **General system flowchart.** A visual presentation of the system at top level. The purpose of this flowchart is to give management a pictorial overview of a particular computer system. The general system flowchart can be presented in the conventional form (Figure 3), or it can be displayed in a more unorthodox form (Figure 4).
- **Functional flowchart.** A visual presentation of the system, subsystem, or program, showing the functions of data with no decision factors or other variables to distract the viewer. The purpose of this flowchart is to synthesize the functions of a system or an application program (Figure 5).
- **Logic flowchart.** A visual presentation of the flow of data through a subsystem and/or program, the location of decision processes, and the control of logic through switching or complicated decision processes. The purpose of this flowchart is to reduce the time required for coding and debugging programs (Figure 6).
- **Hardware configurations flowchart.** A visual presentation of a particular system or facility's hardware. If possible, it should be on one page. The purpose of this flowchart is to provide an overview of a DP facility's or a computer system's hardware (Figure 7).
- **Job step flowchart.** A visual presentation of a computer processing operation. A job step (sometimes called job stream) may consist of one or more programs that process all input and generate all output related to one specific phase of an application, for example, accounts receivable transaction listing (Figure 8). The purpose of this flowchart is to give the operations staff a one-page, all-inclusive visual reference for running a particular job on the computer.
- **Work flowchart.** A visual presentation of the flow of paper or manual work. The purpose of this flowchart is to show in proper sequence the procedures employed by the clerical staff and/or other personnel in preparing and processing a specific application, for example, sales orders for computer operations (Figure 9).

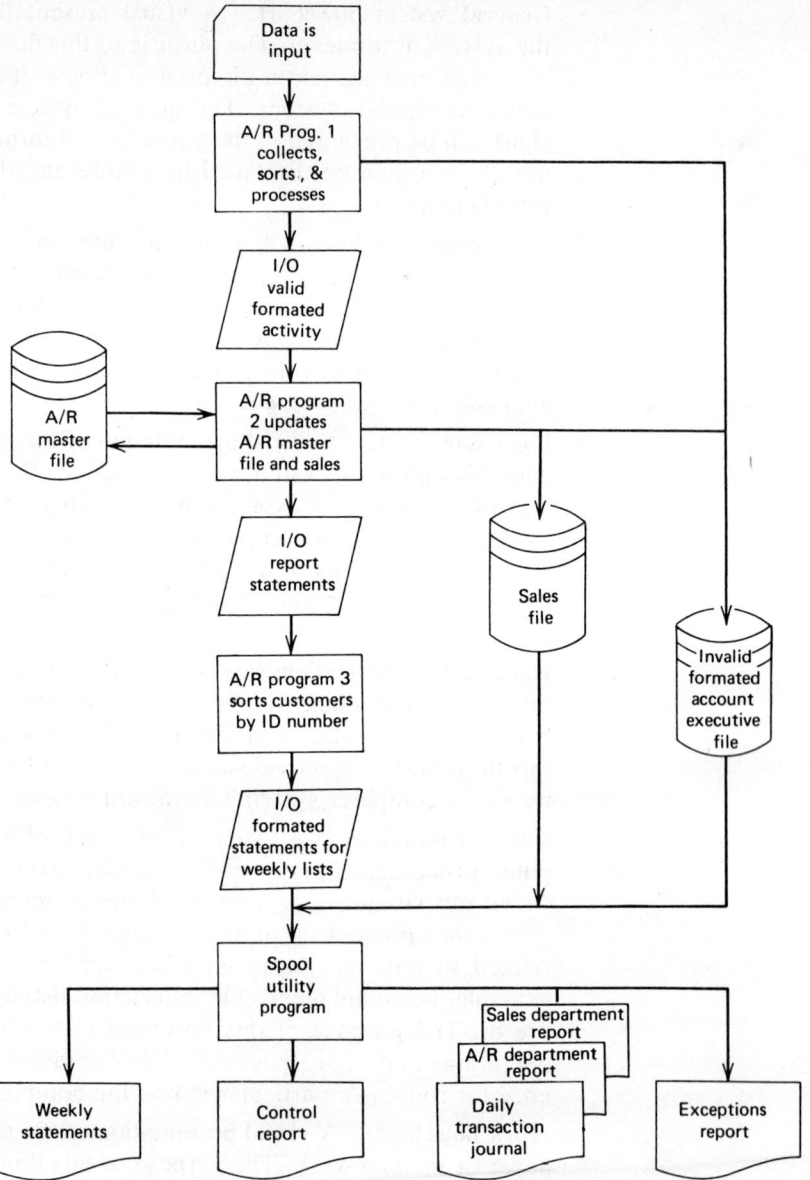

Figure 3. Sample: General system flowchart. Account receivable. Asterisk indicates source documents returned to data control for 60-day retention.

Charts

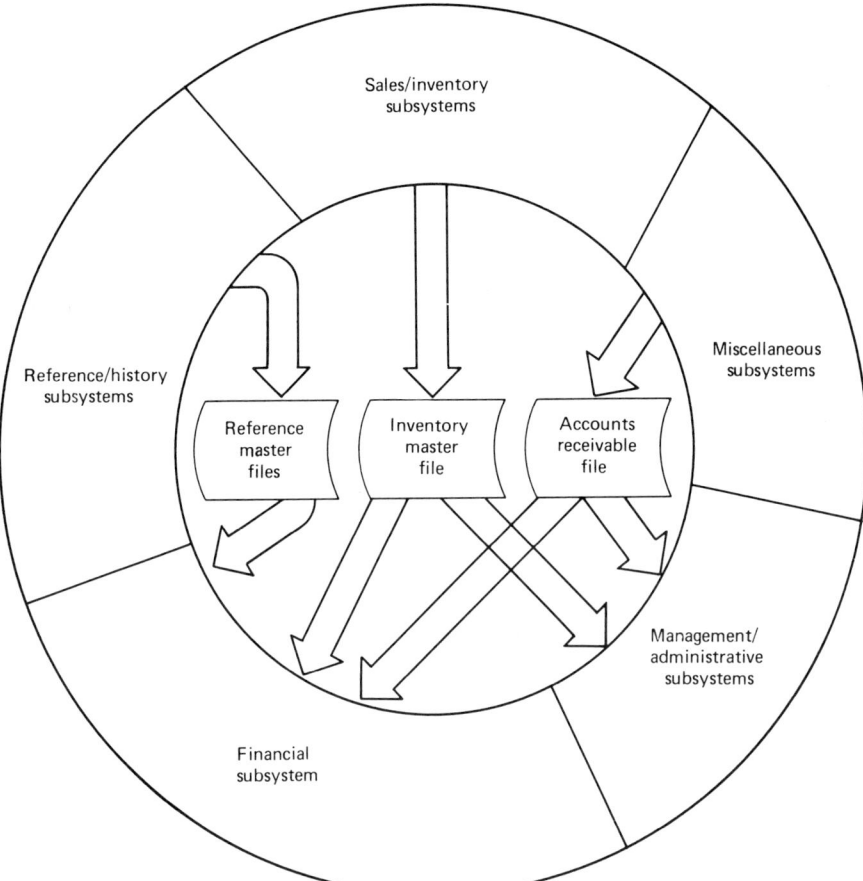

Figure 4. Sample: Management information system. General system flowchart.

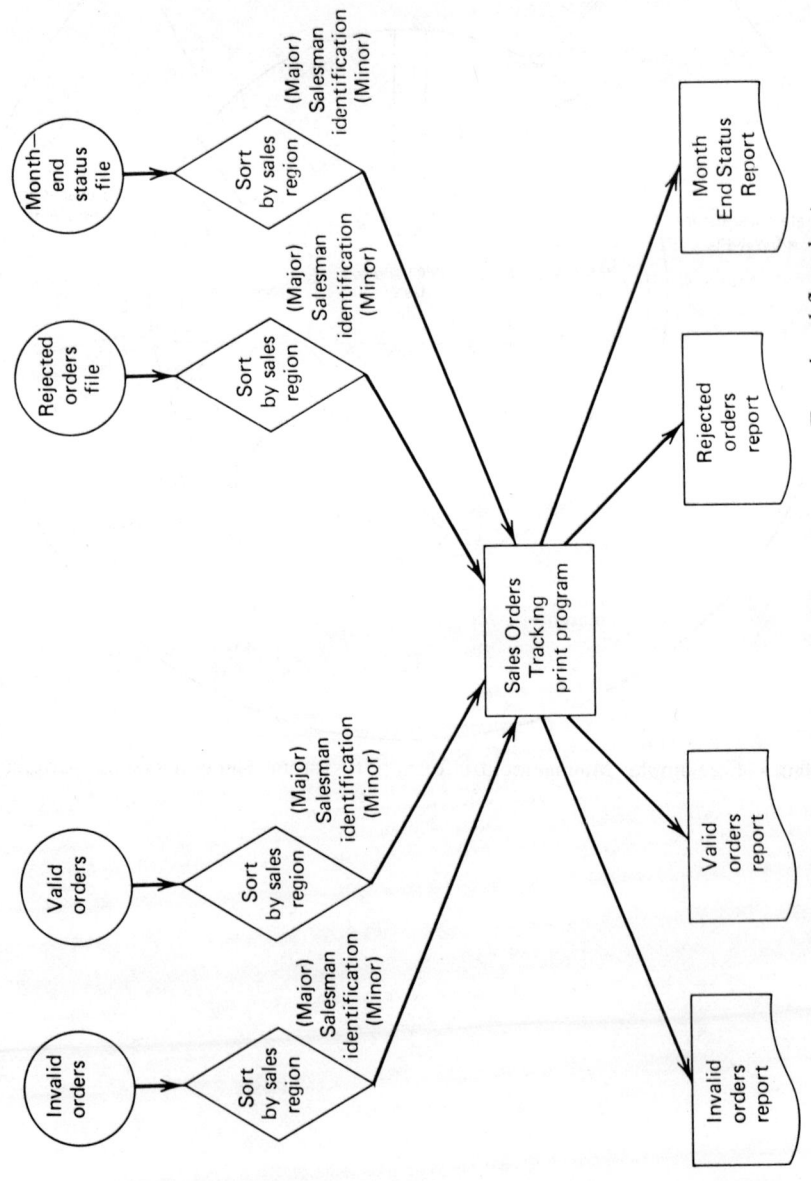

Figure 5. Sample: Sales inventory subsystem. Functional flowchart.

Charts

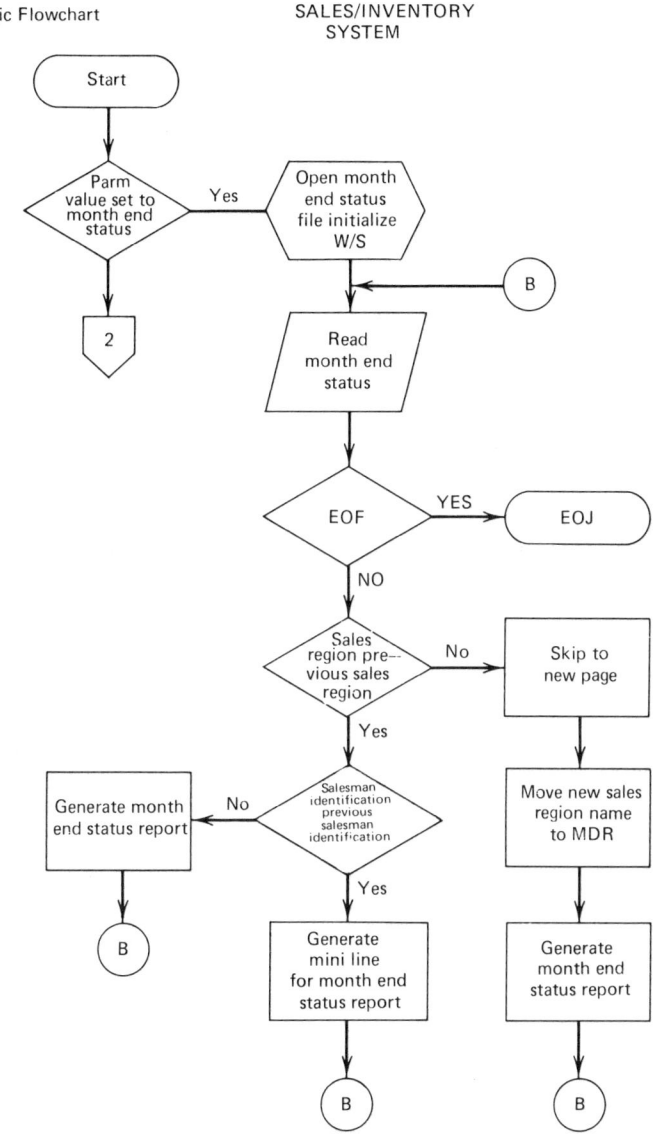

Figure 6. Sample: Logic flowchart.

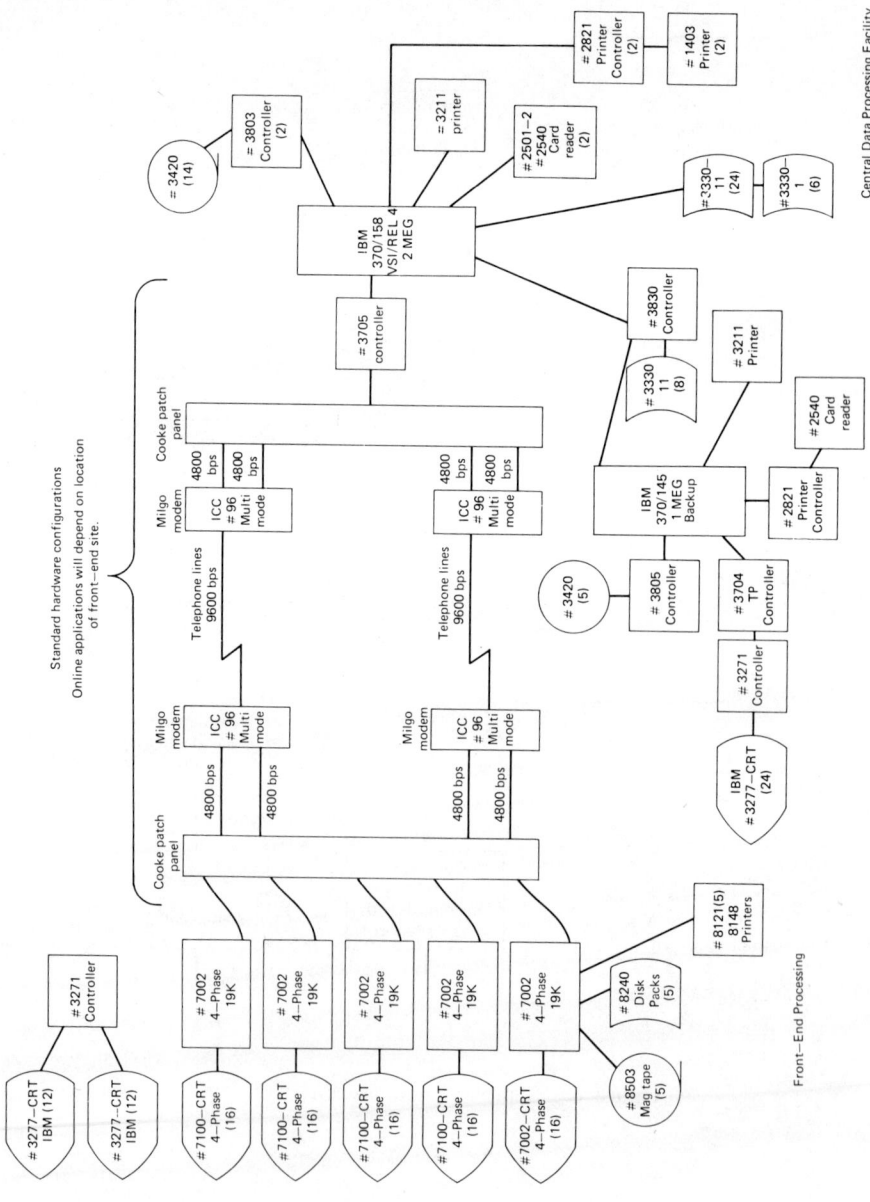

Figure 7. Sample: Standard hardware configurations.

Charts

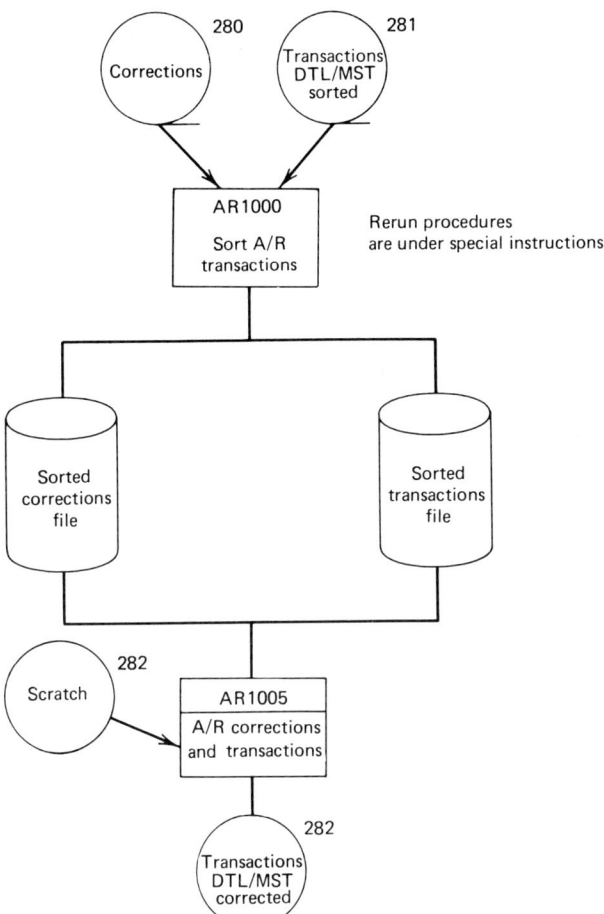

Figure 8. Sample: Job step flowchart.

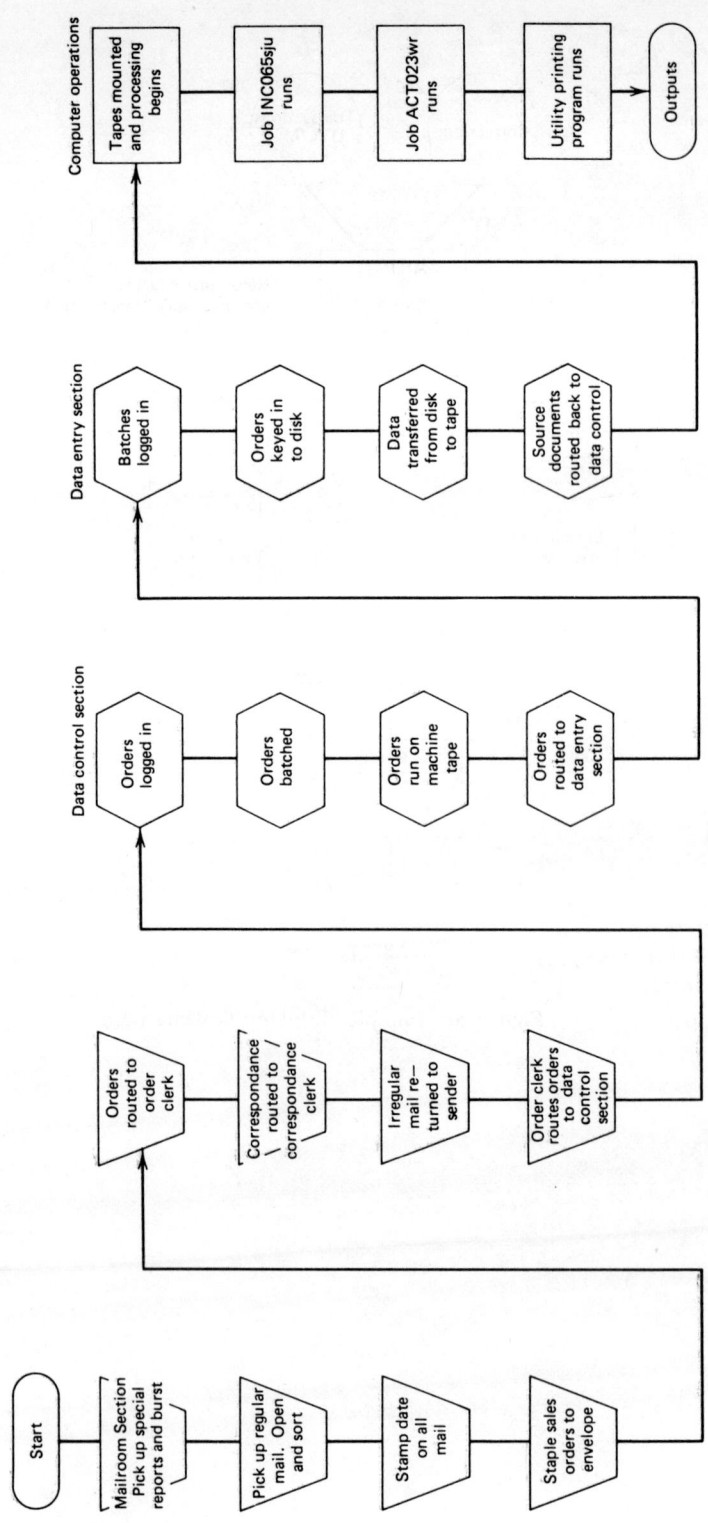

Figure 9. Sample: Work flowchart.

Charts

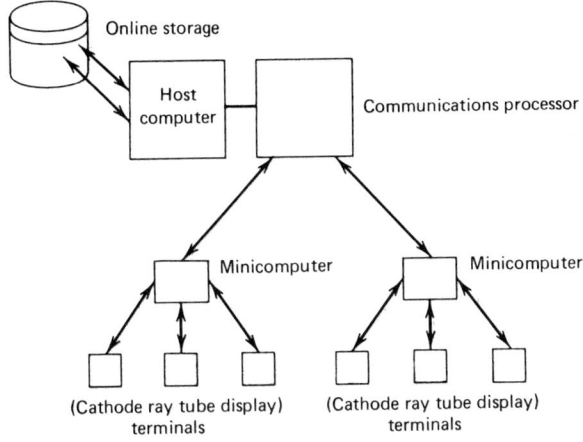

Figure 10. Sample diagram: Simplified view of a hierarchical distributed data processing system. Asterisk indicates cathode ray tube (CRT) display terminals.

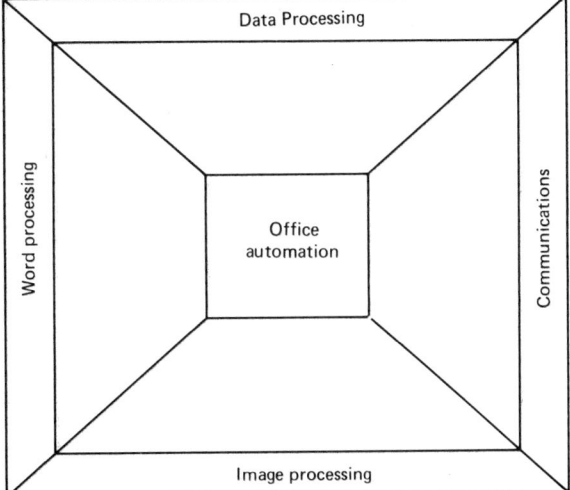

Figure 11. Sample diagram: Simplified presentation of components to effect office automation.

DIAGRAMS SERVE MANY PURPOSES

b. **Diagrams.** Because diagrams are easy to draw and serve well the purpose of presenting anything from an enterprise's profile to a system's structure and operational scheduling simply and clearly, they are the most popular of all manual charts. A case in point is Figure 10, a simplified view of a hierarchical type of distributed data processing system. This type of diagram may be at one end of the spectrum. Figure 11, a simplistic but effective overview of the components that make up office automation, may be at the other end of the spectrum.

TABLES PROVIDE DEFINITIVE INFORMATION

2. TABLES

Of the many graphic tables in use, perhaps the best known are: the decision table, the manloading/scheduling table, and the activity table.

- **Decision table** specifies flow control, and presents the interrelation and interaction of key elements and conditions of decision logic in a system or program. Simply put, the decision table gives a detailed account of all causes and effects in a simple or complicated decision process. The purpose of the decision table is to assist decision making by displaying all possible conditions and the resulting actions (Figure 12).

- **Manloading/Scheduling table** presents the resources and time required for a particular project. It defines the types of personnel needed, for example, supervisory and clerical staffs. It also specifies the time to be spent on hiring and training new hires, and the time employees can spend on specific tasks (Figure 13).

		1	2	3	4	5	6	7	8	9	10	11	12	13	14
Condition stubs	Customer			X											
	Pay history		X												
	Product							X							
	Credit						X								
	Clearance	X													
Action stubs	Discount										X				
	Approve order	X													
	Invalid order						—								
	Reject order									—					
	Terms												X		

Figure 12. Sample: Decision table.

Number	Activity Description	Labor category					1	2	3	4	5	6	7	8	9	10	11	12	13	14	15	16	17	18	19	20	21	22	23	24	25
		1	2	3	4	5																									
1	Hire supervisory staff	5	5				⊢——⊣																								
2	Hire full staff	10	10						⊢——⊣																						
3	Train supervisors		5							⊢⊣																					
4	Train clerical staff		15							⊢——⊣																					
5	Prepare internal opinions manual		10		5						⊢———⊣																				

Figure 13. Sample: Manloading/scheduling table.

- **Activity table** displays the estimated time a particular project will take. The project is broken down into phases such as general system design, detail system design, program specifications, program/system testing, installation/conversion/user training, documentation, and delivery, if the project is the development or conversion of a computer system (Figure 14). Two additional though different activity/milestone methods in wide usage are: CPM (Critical Path Method) and PERT (Project Evaluation Review Technique). To give the reader an idea of what CPM and PERT look like, a sample of each follows (Figures 15 and 16).

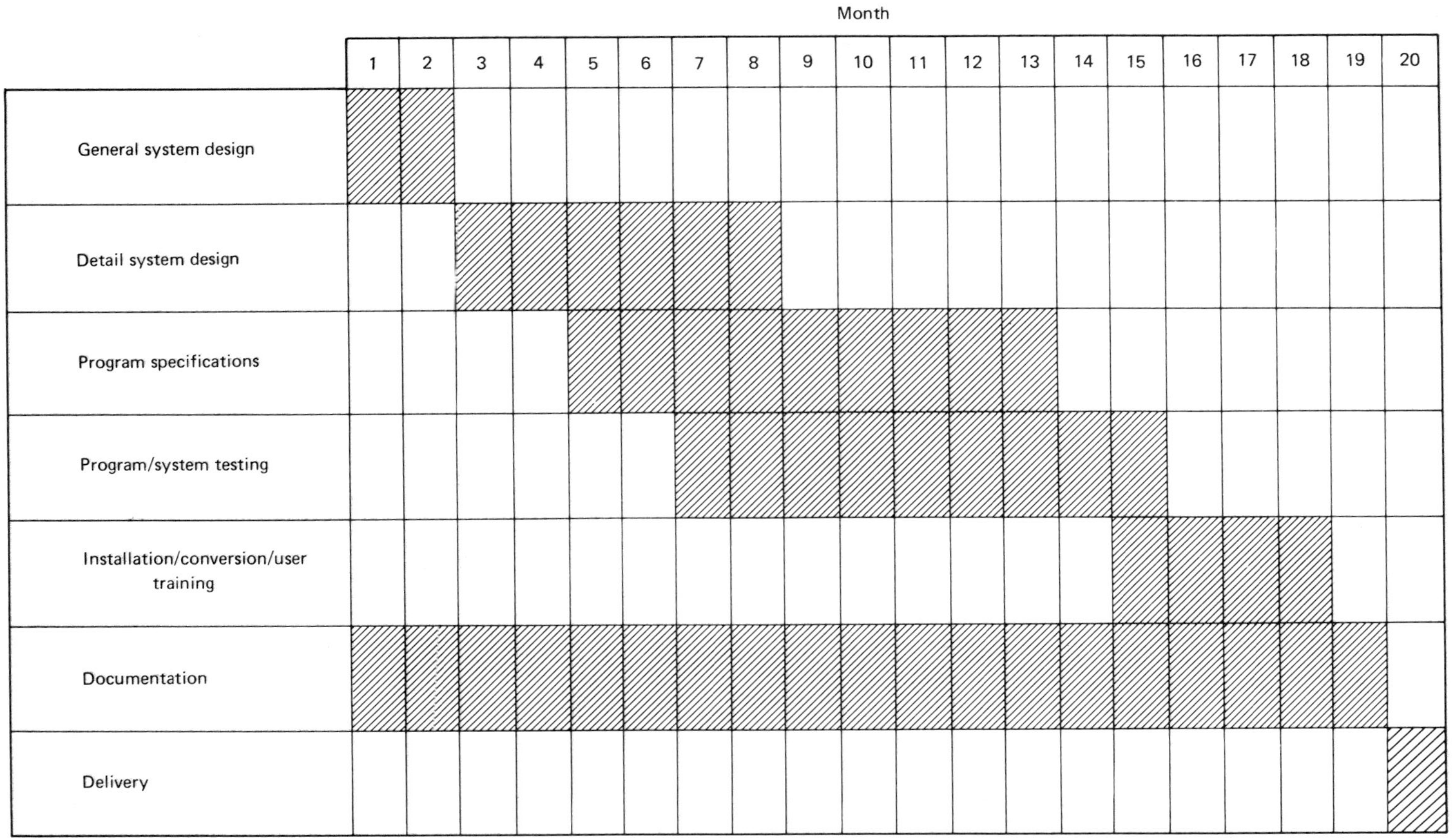

Figure 14. Sample: Time/activity table.

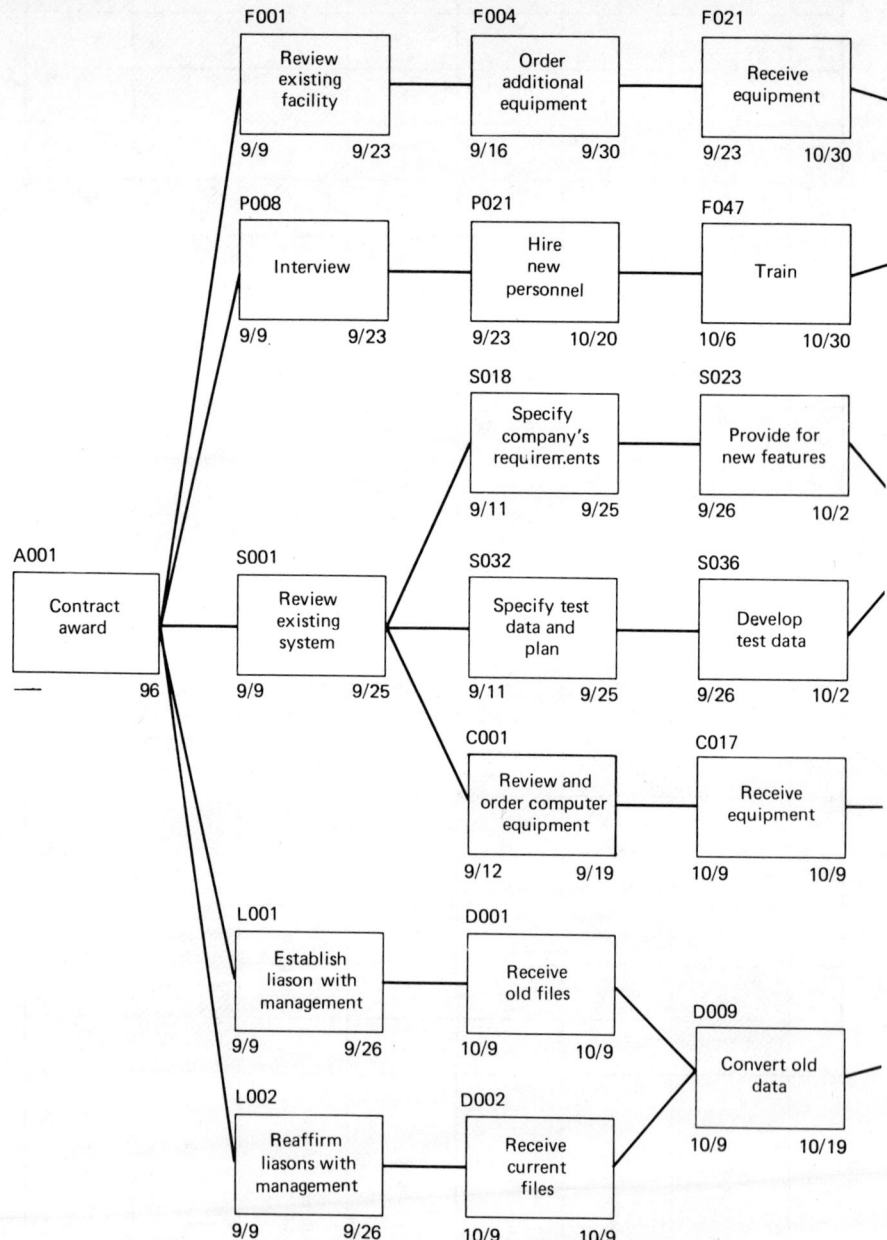

Figure 15. Sample: Critical path

Tables

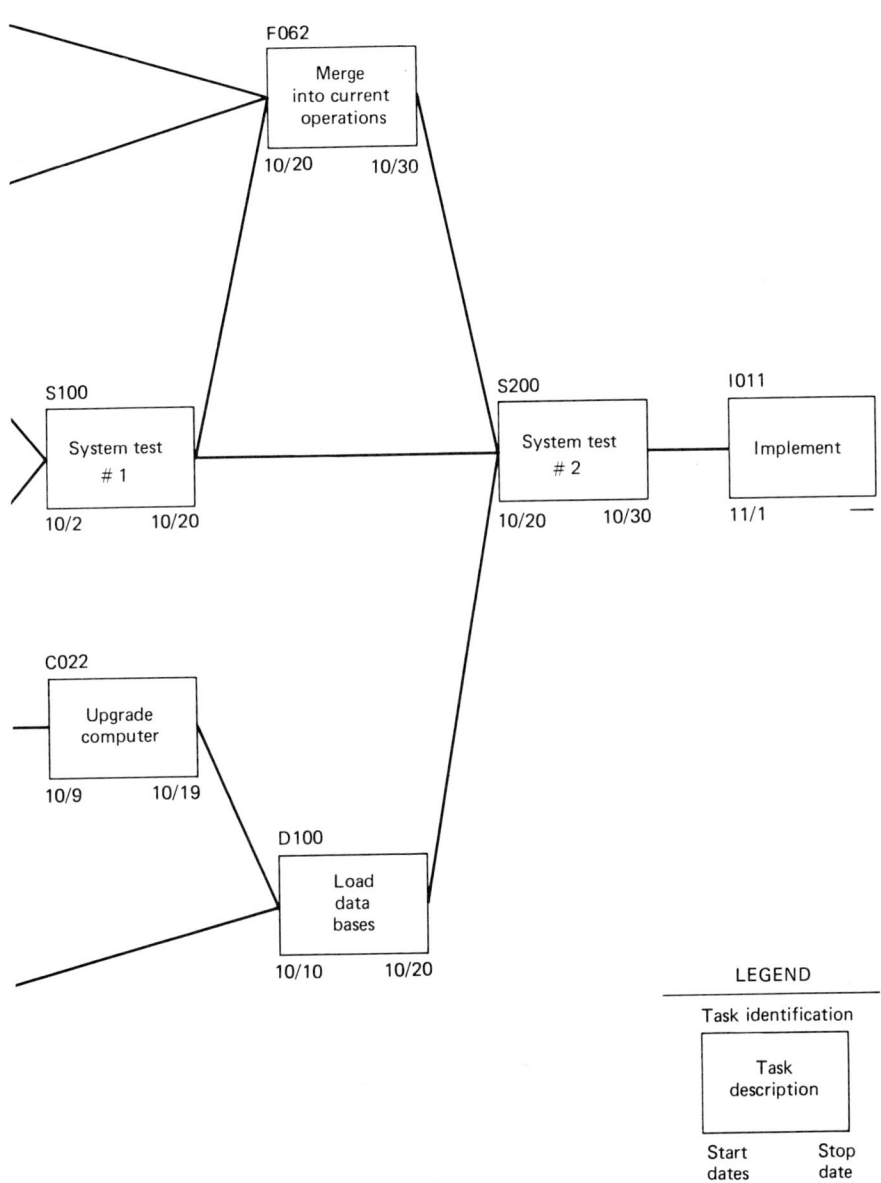

method (CPM) chart.

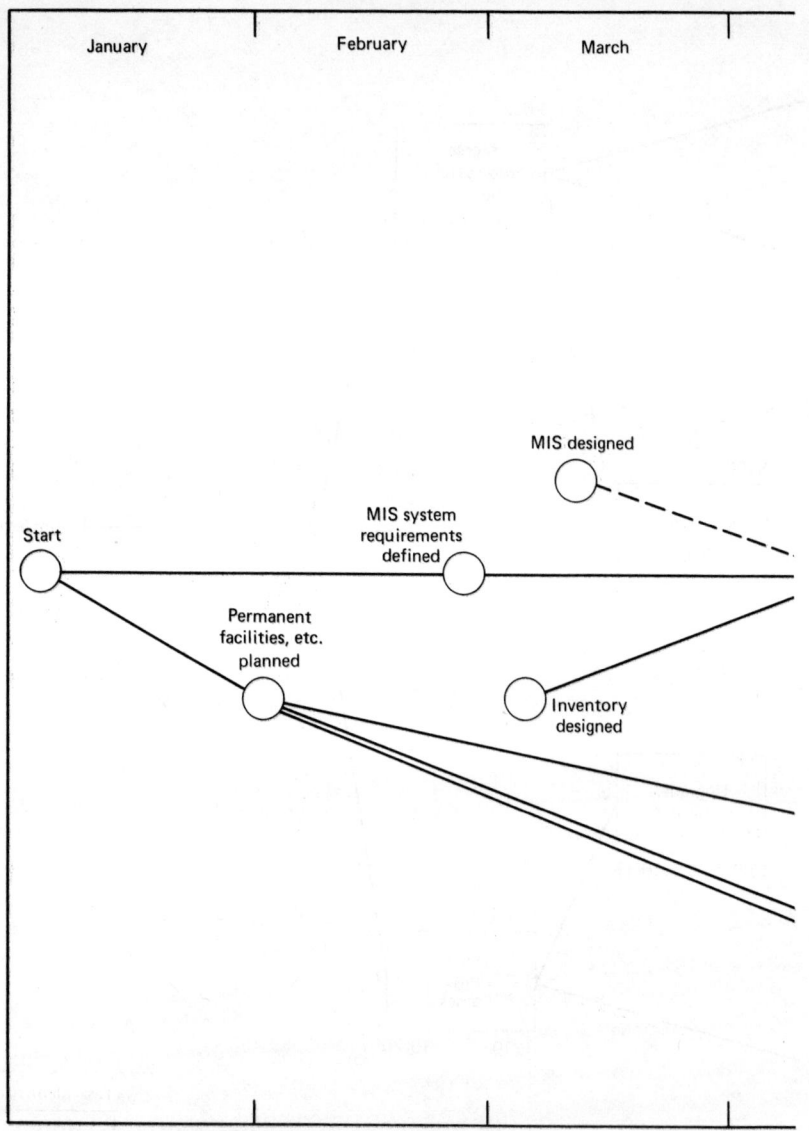

Figure 16. Sample: Project evaluation review technique (PERT) chart. MIS = Man-

Tables

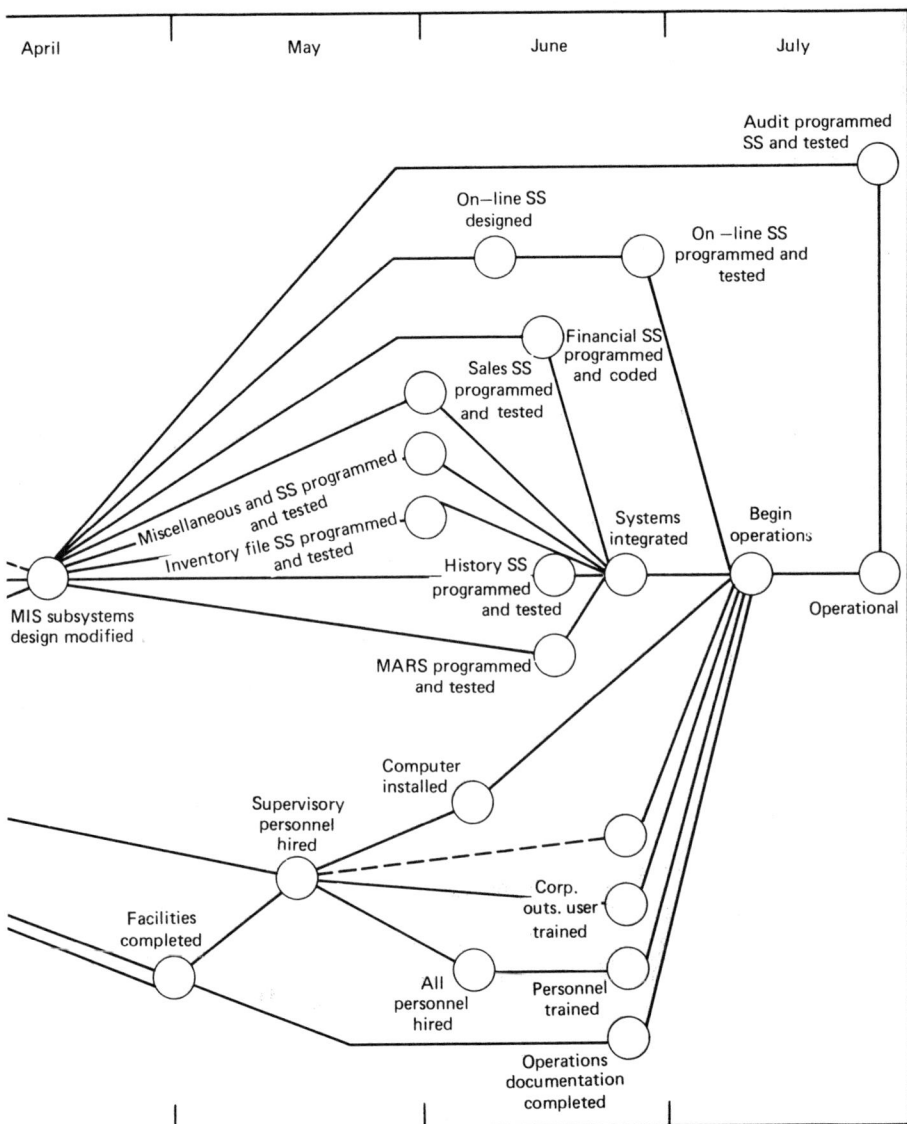

agement information system implementation. SS = Subsystem.

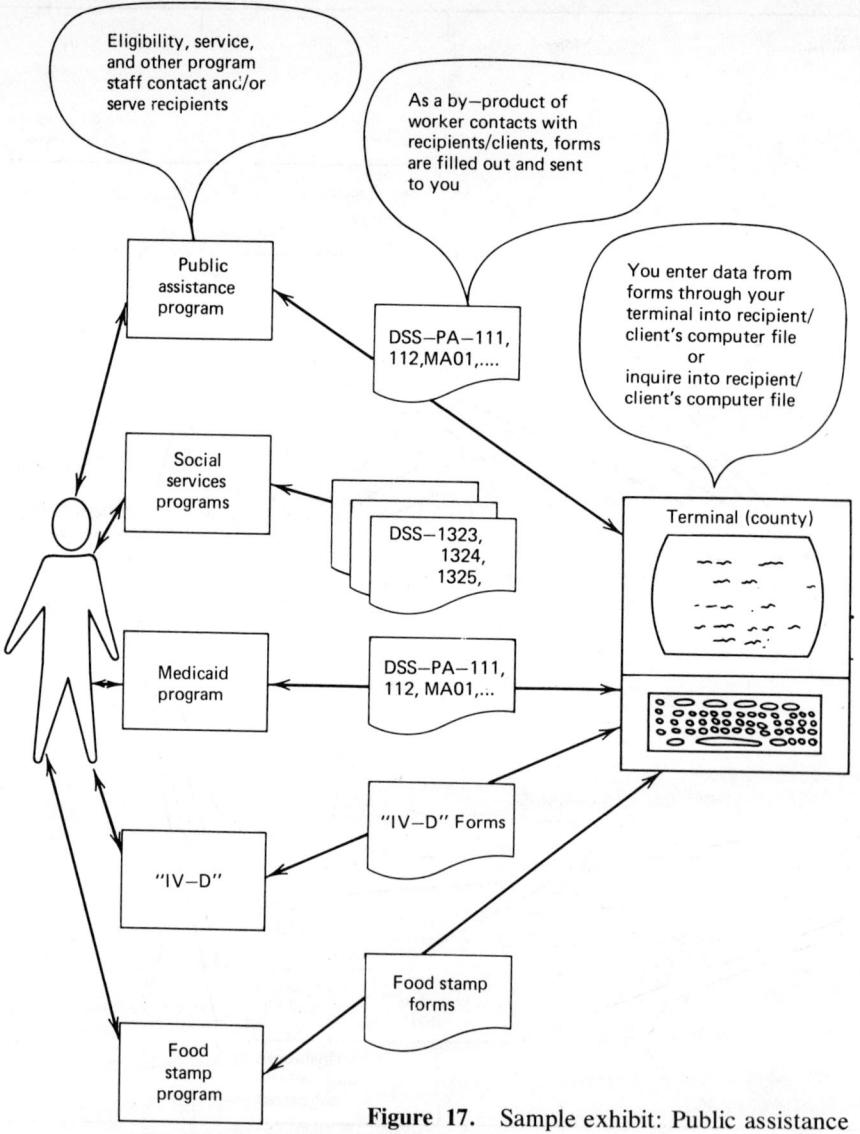

Figure 17. Sample exhibit: Public assistance

EXHIBITS ENHANCE YOUR DOCUMENT

3. EXHIBITS

Exhibits cover a multitude of different types and forms of pictorial presentations. They can be anything from a photograph to a drawing, or a combination of media. For example, the exhibit in Figure 17 uses flowchart symbols,

Exhibits

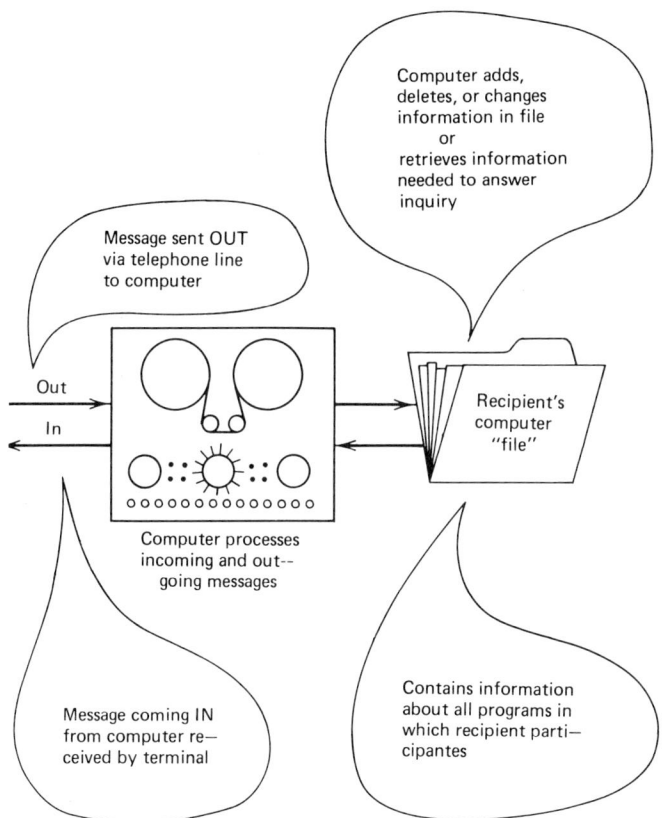

on-line system.

simple drawings, and descriptive labels enclosed in cartoonists' balloons to give non-DP personnel a clear and simple picture of a rather complicated computer system.

Your exhibits are much more effective if your project budget allows you to employ color. If you are working on a tight budget, of course, expensive color illustrations are out of question. In such cases, if at all possible use black-and-white exhibits. The reason is simple: exhibits, whether color or black-and-white, enhance your document and make it more readable.

4. GRAPHICAL DOCUMENTATION

The two major graphical documentation techniques currently in use are: HIPO and SADT. A summary of each methodology with illustrations follows.

a. HIPO. Hierarchy, plus Input, Process, and Output (HIPO) is an IBM-originated method of documentation. It explores the premise that the purposes and subpurposes of a system or application can be graphically presented in terms of functions that convert a series of inputs into a series of outputs. By using HIPO, you can present in a hierarchical structure a set of inputs, the processes that those inputs go through, and the resulting outputs.

HIPO IS AN EFFICIENT DOCUMENTATION TECHNIQUE

Stated simply, HIPO "sees" a system/application as a hierarchy of functions and subfunctions. And in accordance with this concept, it describes and redescribes the particular system/application at succeeding levels of detail. Working examples of HIPO are Figure 18a, which illustrates the top level (overview) functions of a system, and Figure 18b, which displays functions of the same system at the next, more detailed level.

The advantage of this graphic tool is that it helps you to understand the system by illustrating its functional structure. Moreover, a set of HIPO diagrams is effective because they present processing functions such as "open files," "validate sales order," "verify customer credit," and "calculate payroll," in simple and clear form, usually on one page.

Finally, because HIPO is used both in the design and the development phases, documentation is not an "afterthought" task at the end of the project but an ongoing, integral activity.

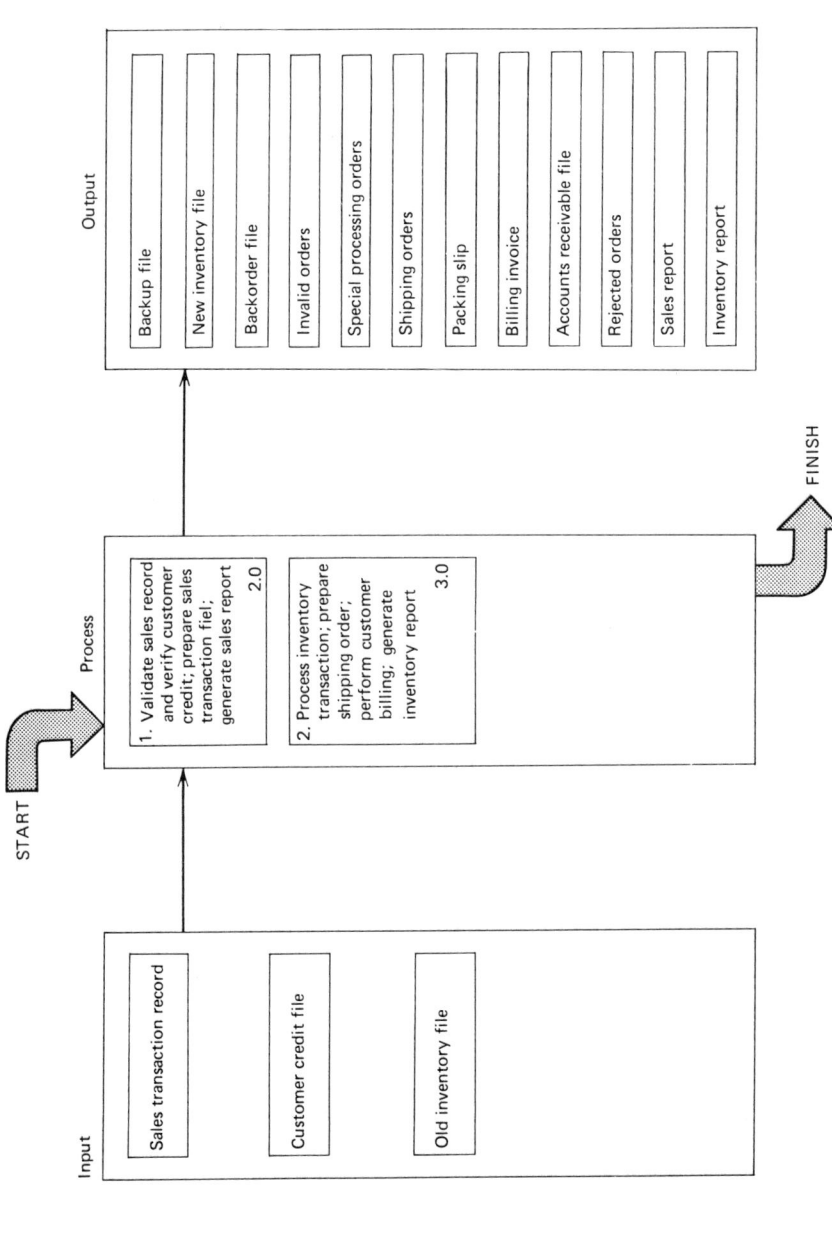

Figure 18a. Sample: Graphical documentation technique—hierarchy, plus input, process and output (HIPO). Sales/inventory system—top level functions.

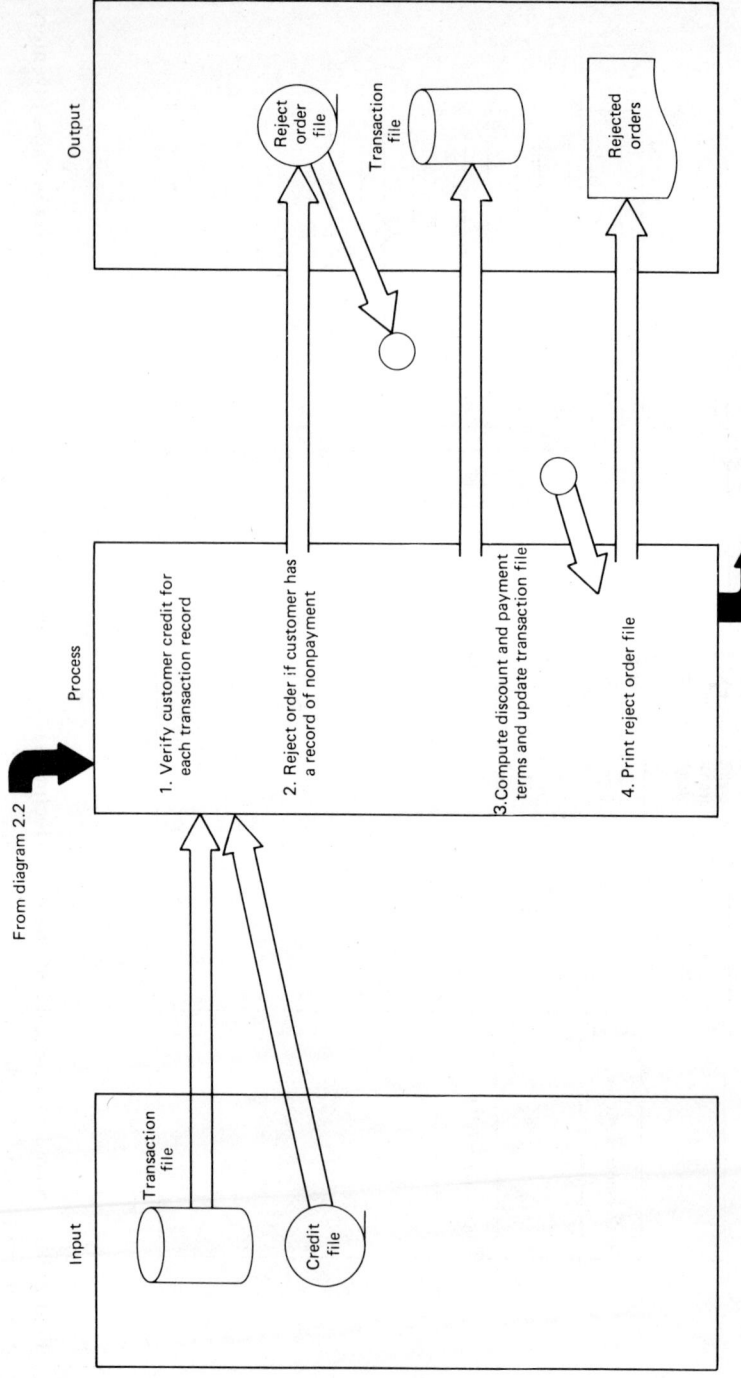

Figure 18b. Sample: HIPO (continued). Sales/inventory system. (Next, more detailed level functions.)

Graphical Documentation

THE LARGE WHITE ARROWS INDICATE THE FLOW OF DATA; THE LARGE DARK ARROWS INDICATE THE FLOW OF CONTROL

A HIPO package consists of many diagrams starting with the very useful visual table of contents (Figure 19). This diagram is a directory, indicating the locations of all the diagrams in the package. It also serves as a legend, pointing out the roles and meanings of different arrows on the diagrams.

The large white arrows between the input and process blocks, and between the process and output blocks, indicate the *flow of data;* while the large dark arrows show the *flow of control* in the project.

To be more precise, the large dark arrows symbolize entry and exit from the diagrams. Thus, a dark arrow at the top shows you the preceding diagram; while the dark arrow at the bottom directs you to the next diagram in the series.

The large white arrows symbolize movement or flow of data, or reference a data item. They point from input to process, from process to output, and from output back to process. These arrows, however, NEVER point from process back to input.

Moreover, each diagram references subordinate diagrams, leaving no margin for misunderstanding. As Figure 19 indicates, each box in the hierarchy diagram (i.e., the functional diagram of the system) contains a title or heading, and the number of the diagram in the series that describes the function. In addition, there is a description section that expands on the titles and headings in the hierarchy diagram.

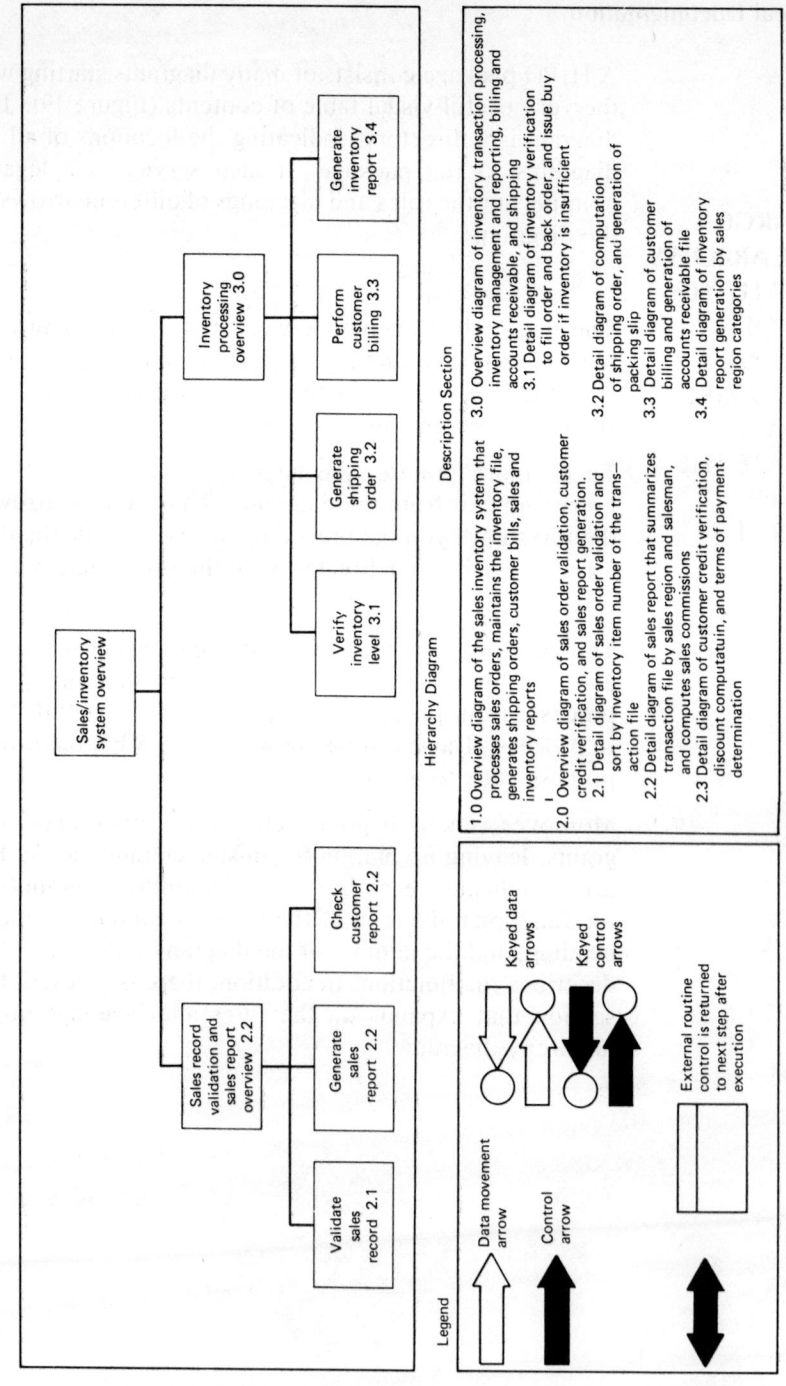

Figure 19. Sample: HIPO (continued). Sales/inventory system. Table of contents.

Graphical Documentation

THE ROLES OF THE HIERARCHY AND DETAIL HIPO DIAGRAMS ARE QUITE DIFFERENT

Although the overview and detail HIPO diagrams are graphically identical, or at least similar, their purposes are different. The hierarchy diagram provides an overview of a system, application, or function. Thus, if the manager or auditor wants to know "What is the purpose of the system?," the overview (top level) diagram of HIPO will provide the answer. On the other hand, the detail diagram provides definitive information about a particular function. Thus, if the analyst, programmer, DP auditor, or user wants to know "What is this program doing?," the detail diagram supplies the answer.

In sum, HIPO provides a precise graphic documentation through its overview and its subsequent detailed diagrams in hierarchical sequence. It can best be utilized in the design and development phases of computer systems. It can also be used in certain procedures such as data entry, data control, or computer operations.

SADT IS A PROBLEM DEFINITION DOCUMENTATION TECHNIQUE

b. SADT.* Structure Analysis and Design Technique (SADT) is a top-down, modular, problem definition-oriented graphical documentation tool developed by SofTech Company, Waltham, Massachusetts. The SADT diagrams describe the system in relation to its activities and to its data.

Specifically, models of systems are displayed in terms of entities (objects or data), and in terms of happenings (activities performed by people, equipment, computer, software, etc.).

The activity and data or objects of a system are studied in relationship to each other (Figure 20). Thus boxes in the "activity" diagram focus on activities (verbs), and arrows in that diagram represent data (nouns). Conversely, boxes in the "data" diagram focus on entities (nouns), and arrows in that diagram represent activities (verbs).

---

*SADT is a Trademark of SofTech Company, Inc., Waltham, MA 02154.

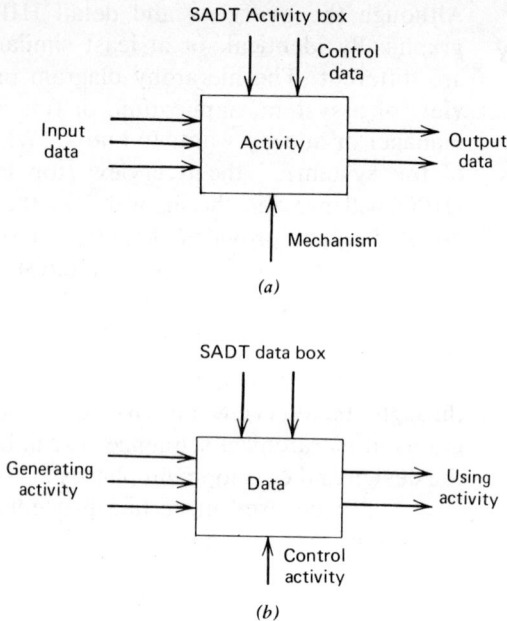

Figure 20. Sample: Graphical documentation technique—structure analysis and design technique (SADT) (a) SADT activity box (b) SADT data box.

The SADT diagrams or modules are composed of boxes with connecting arrows. These "logical decomposition" boxes are arranged in a hierarchy, leading to more and more detail. Specifically, an entire diagram, contained on a 8½ × 11 inch page, is divided into *not less* than three "activity" boxes, and *not more* than six boxes (Figure 21).

SADT DIAGRAMS ARE COMPOSED OF BOXES WITH CONNECTING ARROWS

Point in fact: each box represents only one activity, and consequently, if it takes more than six boxes to decompose an activity (i.e., to explain in detail the activity of one box from a higher level diagram), either you have gone into too much detail too soon, or the higher level diagram does not have enough detail.

The first SADT diagram is a functional model in the earliest stage of system development. This model shows "what the problem is." The next diagram is a design

Graphical Documentation

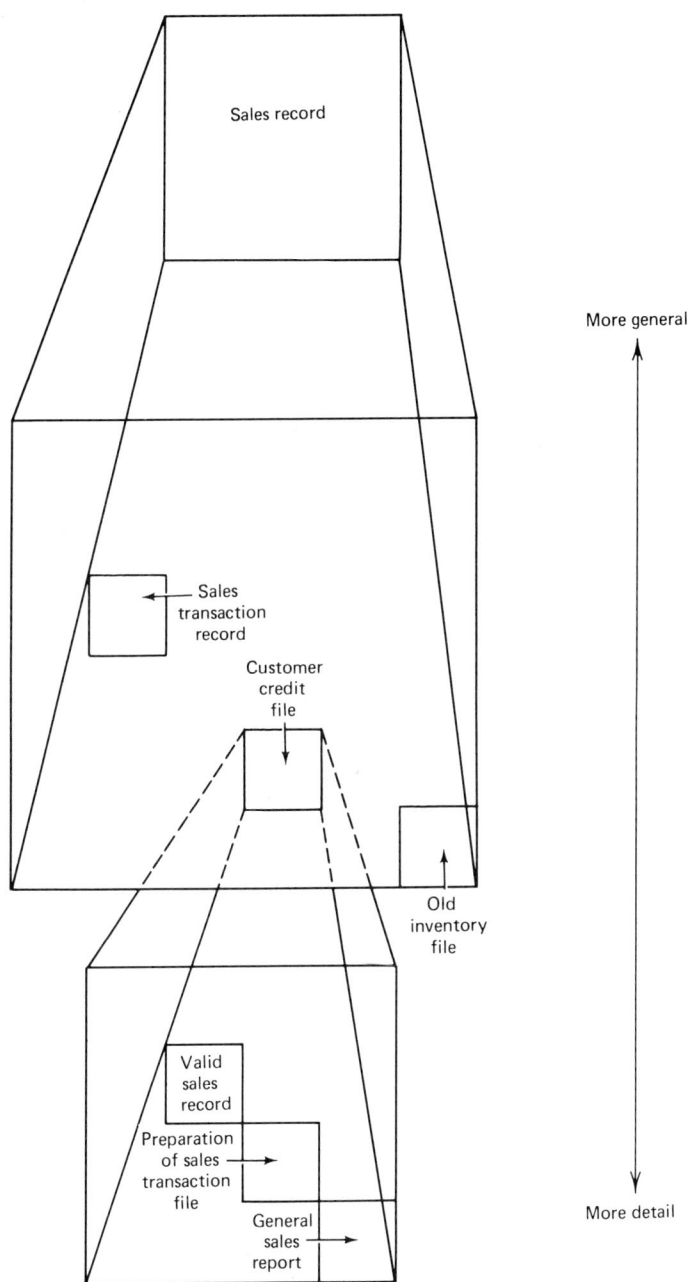

Figure 21. Sample: SADT (continued). Sales/inventory system. Model building via structured decomposition.

model of "how the problem will be solved," that is, what approach might solve the problem, and indeed whether automation is the answer.

SADT makes it possible to make up one functional model representing the viewpoint of the systems analyst/designer, and one representing the user's viewpoint. These two models are then cross-referenced for a thorough understanding of the stated problem.

In addition, the diagrams are reviewed at certain predefined checkpoints by the user as well as analysts working on other projects. This is to ensure that the problem, the system requirements, and the system development models are in accord with the user's need. Each time some aspect of the system is changed, the diagrams are changed to reflect the latest decision.

A great advantage of this graphical tool is that contrary to conventional flowcharts, SADT has no formal symbols to indicate steps and data in control flow. The fact is that standard DP symbols tend to distract or confuse a person, especially a non-DP person, trying to read a conventional flowchart.

Also, the arrows, unlike those in HIPO and other documentation methods, are quite simple (Figure 22). Further, the point at which they enter or leave an activity box is important; the shape of the arrow is not.

Arrows indicating INPUT come into the left side of the box; arrows indicating OUTPUT leave on the right. Within diagrams, the arrows connecting the boxes show how these components interrelate. External control factors such as "Current Price" or "Last Day of the Month" are indicated by arrows coming into the *top of the box;* the processor or device that performs the activity or stores the data is called "mechanism arrow," and it comes into the box from the *bottom*.

Output from one activity may become the input or the controlling factor for another activity. Moreover, language used in SADT diagrams is simple and nontechnical.

Graphical Documentation

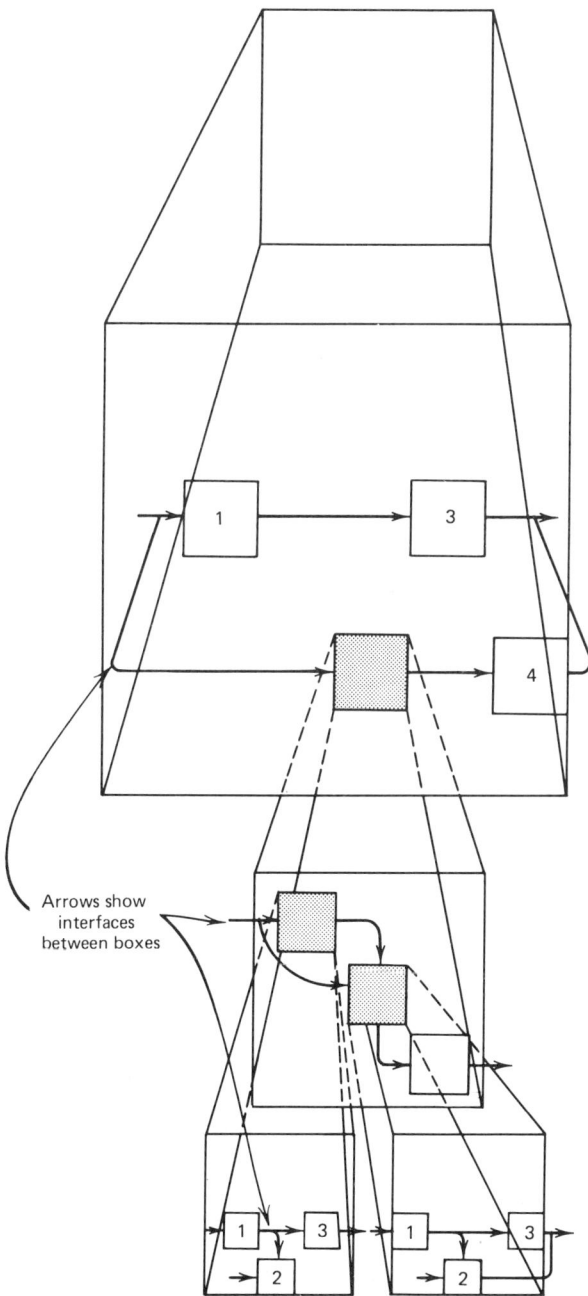

Figure 22. Sample: SADT (continued). Arrow interfaces.

SADT DIAGRAMS PRESENT MORE AND MORE DETAILS IN A STRUCTURED MANNER

In sum, SADT is a top-down hierarchy sequence of diagrams, accompanied by brief descriptive labels. The high-level diagram is an overview of the subject, and each subsequent lower-level diagram exposes more and more detail in a structured manner. SADT is best utilized in the analysis and design phases of systems development, as well as in the analysis and problem definition phases of systems' modifications during their life cycles.

PART TWO
Writing System-Related Documents

Chapter Six
Writing Effective Progress Reports

Progress reports don't have to be boring, long-winded, or pointless. You can present a narrative on the progress of a project concisely and interestingly. By adopting commercial newspaper and magazine writing techniques, you can catch the reader's attention with the very first paragraph, with the very first sentence. If your summary, which precedes the body of your report, gives a coherent overview of the progress (or lack of progress) of the assignment in a clear, vivid style, there's less likelihood of encountering management disinterest or significant delay in reading it. Moreover, you have a much better chance of getting a positive response to such a document than to one of those traditional, dull, pompous progress reports. At this point, it is important to clear up a widespread misconception in the DP field about "status" report and "progress" report.

- **Status report** identifies the state or condition of a project in development, and measures established in systems performance criteria, scope, justification, and acceptability. In other words, a status report describes the project viability in regard to significant variances (if there are any) from planned specifications. These include initial time and cost estimates, and quality criteria, and offers recommendations to resolve problems (if there are any).
- **Progress report,** on the other hand, presents the actual accomplished phases in a study/analysis, task/assignment, planning/development, or conversion/implementation of a project.

Both of these reports are powerful communication tools. Properly prepared, they can save considerable sums of money for the DP facility and for the enterprise.

DRESS UP YOUR REPORT

1. FRONT SECTION

When you want to communicate, it helps to "package" your report as attractively as possible, without being ostentatious or running into extra expenses. Packaging starts with the cover, which may be clear plastic, colored plastic, or cardboard. Next is the title page, followed by a well-organized table of contents and a list of illustrations. The report itself should be typed in an easy-to-read typewriter font, error-free, and framed by generous margins. These guidelines may be applied to short and long reports, in-house reports, and formal reports that are disseminated outside the organization. Of course, reports that consist of only a few pages need not have a table of contents or a list of illustrations.

a. The title page. Since the title page is the first thing management will glance at, it should provide not only complete identification of the subject, but an indication of the care and effort that went into the preparation of the report. Attractiveness is important here, so be sure that the title, subtitle (if there is one), the name(s) of the author(s), the company (if applicable), the department (if applicable), and the date are attractively arranged. (See title page of the sample progress report at the end of this chapter.)

If the progress report is to be submitted to an outside company or government agency, the title page must identify that organization, and (if appropriate) the person for whom the report is prepared, as well as the contract number, if applicable. In addition, your company's name and address must be displayed on the title page. Moreover, a lot of thought should be given to the title itself. It should be informative yet succinct.

CASE IN POINT

Version 1: "Progress report on the Project of Gathering, Defining, and Organizing Specifications for the Development of a Data Base Management System to be Used in a Formal Request for Proposal."

Version 2: "Progress Report on the Specifications for a Data Base Management System Development Project."

The first version may be accurate and complete, but it's long and tiresome. Moreover, if the title is any indication of the report that follows, pity the poor reader who will have to wade through it. The second version is much shorter yet just as informative as the first one.

b. Table of contents and list of illustrations. The table of contents, or the contents, as it's usually called, presents an outline of the report's content in primary and secondary headings. As a rule, the primary headings (indicating main sections) are typed in capital letters. For example, POTENTIAL PROBLEMS. And the secondary or subheadings are typed in capital and lowercase letters. For example, User Dissatisfaction. The sections may be indicated by Roman or arabic numbers, or by capital letters. The absence of any letter or number is also acceptable. For example:

IV. POTENTIAL PROBLEMS

4. POTENTIAL PROBLEMS

D. POTENTIAL PROBLEMS or

POTENTIAL PROBLEMS

If the major sections are indicated by Roman numerals, the subsections should be indicated by capital letters; and the sub-subsections by arabic numerals. For example:

IV. POTENTIAL PROBLEMS

    A. User Dissatisfaction

        1. Lack of Communication

        2. Obsolete Documentation

If the major sections are indicated by arabic numbers, the subsections may be indicated by capital letters, or you may use the military specifications or "MIL-SPECS" method of extending the main section number another two digits.

The subsections in these two cases are indicated by the lowercase letters and by three digits, respectively. For example:

4. POTENTIAL PROBLEMS
    A. User Dissatisfaction
        a. Lack of Communication
        b. Obsolete Documentation

or

4. POTENTIAL PROBLEMS
    4.1 User Dissatisfaction
        4.1.1 Lack of Communication
        4.1.2 Obsolete Documentation

Of course, if no numerals or capital letters precede the major headings, no numerals or letters precede subheadings either, and you indicate subitems just by indentation. For example:

POTENTIAL PROBLEMS
    User Dissatisfaction
        Lack of Communication
        Obsolete Documentation

The list of illustrations, or simply illustrations, follows the contents page. It lists in sequential order all figures, charts, tables, and exhibits contained in the progress report. As a rule, there are three columns on the illustrations page. For example:

ILLUSTRATIONS

Figure	Title	Page
1	User Department Work Flow Diagram	10
2	Decision Table	12

If there are only a couple of charts or tables in the report, there is no need to waste a whole page. The figures can be listed on the contents page, immediately following the last item.

SUMMARY IS THE "SHOWCASE" OF YOUR REPORT

2. SUMMARY

The summary that introduces the body of a progress report is the "showcase" part of the report. It is designed for the busy executive who wants to read only the highlights of the subject matter. Another, perhaps more important objective of the summary is to "entice" the same busy executive to flip that page and read through the entire report. (It's to your advantage that management knows the details of your progress and the problems you've encountered as soon as possible, so that appropriate action can be taken.) Consequently, when writing the summary, be frugal and stick to essentials only. However, this does not necessarily mean dull, dry sentences. Try to follow the "attention-grabber" methods of newspaper and magazine articles, and you will increase the chances of arousing management's interest in your report. Of course, it goes without saying that the most polished techniques won't "sell" a report unless there is substance to it.

CASE IN POINT

Version 1: "This paper is a report on the progress made by the task force, appointed by management to study and recommend alternatives for the company's inventory system, which is faced with several problems created by the methods with which information is gathered and processed, and which could no longer be left unaddressed."

Version 2: "A breakthrough was effected by the management-appointed task force in the study and recommendation of alternative methods to improve the antiquated information modes of the company's inventory system."

Which version do you think will catch management's attention? Not only is version 2 direct and positive, but it contains only 27 words, whereas version 1 rambles on for 50 words.

SET THE TONE OF YOUR REPORT IN THE SUMMARY

Stated differently, by writing a strong, positive summary of your or your team's progress, you put the reader in an affirmative mood. Conversely, if there is no significant progress to report, you point this out in the very first sentence of the summary. This is to set the stage and thus prepare the reader for a negative report. Consider these two examples:

It is disappointing to report that the task force has not achieved its stated goal during the past month in the development of a data dictionary system.

And

Because of the many unforeseen problems that the task force had to deal with, progress in finalizing the DBMS specifications during the reporting period has been less than satisfactory.

By boldly stating the lack of progress in the opening sentence, you avoid any possible accusations of covering up or holding back information about an unpleasant situation. Moreover, you may arouse the interest and concern of the executive. Consequently, he or she may read the full report, and perhaps do something about resolving the problems that are delaying or even stopping the progression of a task.

The main thing in writing a summary is to be aware of the power of this device, and to fully utilize it. Specifically, you can create a positive or negative atmosphere (depending on the effect you intend to achieve) with your opening sentence.

Once you have set the stage for the type of progress report you plan to present, complete your summary. It should include a brief overview of the subject, a sentence or two on the scope of work, and finally a succinct statement about the scheduled work to be covered in the next progress report (if there's one) due on a given date.

MAKE YOUR INTRODUCTION AS CONCISE AS POSSIBLE

3. INTRODUCTION

Since the introduction is the bridge that takes the reader from the summary to the discussion or body of the prog-

Conclusion

ress report, make it brief. Include only terse yet complete statements about the period covered by the report, the actual progress (or lack of progress) made in the particular assignment, and the problems faced.

DISCUSSION IS THE "MEAT" OF YOUR REPORT

4. DISCUSSION

The discussion, being a critical part of the progress report, should contain a thorough description of the *principal* activities in which you or your group have been involved. This section supports, reinforces, and details the accomplishments highlighted in the summary. Here you also can elaborate on the difficulties or problems you have met and resolved, as well as any *potential* problems that may arise in the next reporting period.

CAUTION

Do not bring up petty problems though. If you do, you will probably lose the interest and support of management, and you may reduce your credibility as a professional. Management does not want to hear about minor (though perhaps irritating) problems or petty annoyances. They feel, and rightly so, that you, as their subordinate professional staff, should take care of such things without ever mentioning it to them. If this seems like belaboring the obvious, it is. Yet many professionals who should know better, fall into this trap.

IMPORTANT POINT

To effect a smooth, easy-to-read progress report it's essential that all the detailed supporting data do not weigh down and interrupt the flow of your narrative in the discussion. They should be presented in the appendix, for reference.

CONCLUDE YOUR REPORT WITH A BRIEF ACCOUNT OF MAIN POINTS

5. CONCLUSION

In the conclusion section, you repeat briefly the important points presented in the discussion. You also state the scope of projected activities, the schedule of work to be performed within the next predetermined period, and the due-date of the next report.

NOTE: The schedule can serve as a control device when checked both by management and by you or your group against the next progress report, when it appears.

The format, approach, and writing style of the following sample in-house progress report are applicable to status reports as well, except that the latter usually includes a recommendations section.

SAMPLE **Progress Report**

PROGRESS REPORT ON THE SPECIFICATIONS
FOR A NEW HOSPITAL MANAGEMENT
INFORMATION SYSTEM

October 10, 1981

INFORMATION SYSTEMS DEPARTMENT

Jim Green
Bruce Harvey
Marcelo Hoffman
Mark Smith

CONTENTS

Section	Page
SUMMARY	99
I. INTRODUCTION	99
II. DISCUSSION	99
A. Personnel	100
B. Equipment	101
III. CONCLUSION	101

SUMMARY

A major milestone has been reached by the systems development team in the preliminary phase of our project to write a definitive Request For Proposal (RFP) for the new hospital computer system. Specifically, we have been able to define the particular areas that could best utilize a Management Information System (MIS).

Our primary emphasis during this period has been on outlining the functional areas the system must support. The design approach to the system is to be on a modular basis. The system is to be implemented in functional units (modules), with the capability to interchange information across module boundaries. The equipment used will be a large central processor to be specified, with many remote video display terminals for input/output. Details regarding the storage media and the peripheral devices have not yet been addressed. Outside computer professionals, working on a fixed-price contract and under the close supervision of our MIS staff, will do most of the system development work.

We are progressing on schedule, and successful completion of the assignment in the form of a formal RFP is expected by January 1982.

I. INTRODUCTION

Our major thrust since the last progress report (September 3, 1981) has been to detail the specific areas in which a MIS could be most useful and most economical. The criteria outlined in the previous report were applied to evaluate the list of potential uses. These criteria are:

1. The system should provide a fast means of supplying information to the users at their work stations.
2. Paper work should be reduced.
3. Communication between different functions should be substantially improved.

The team evaluated each potential use of the computer against the established criteria, and assigned a priority (a, b, and c) to each one. In this manner we defined the scope of the total system. The hospital system to be detailed in the RFP will contain the performance capabilities listed in the appendix of the next (final) report.

II. DISCUSSION

Our survey of computer systems used by various hospitals in the area shows that the extent of computer usage varies significantly. While some hospitals rely heavily on automated systems, others take a more conservative approach. The two major factors in determining the degree of computer usage are the amount of funds available, and the willingness of the proposed users to accept the systems.

With respect to the first point (funds), we held several discussions with the hospital controller to determine how much financial support might be available for the proposed system. In general, there was a strong commitment to establishing an effective system, while keeping risks low and holding to reasonable costs. Since many aspects of the proposed system promise cost-effective paybacks, constraints were not severely limiting.

The second point (acceptance by users), however, presented some problems. Informal contracts with many of the hospital personnel indicated a strong suspicion of computer systems, and an inherent reluctance to rely on them. Moreover, the same hospital personnel were quick to point to problems in other hospital systems that are attempting elaborate automation.

One trouble area was the storage of the patient care records in the computer. The physicians in particular were not enthusiastic about this aspect of the system because of their need to obtain hard copies of all records at their convenience. We also ascertained that they were not inclined to use the terminal to directly enter medical orders.

As a result of this investigation by the team members, we agreed not to maintain complete patient care records in the computer. Most other paperwork, however, is to be included in the new automated system.

Based on further study and analysis, we concluded that this approach has the following advantages:

1. It offers a higher probability that the system will be used.
2. It allows modularity in construction, since many of the facets of the system have become somewhat independent as a result of the decision not to store patient care records in the computer.
3. The modular approach offers the opportunity to introduce features of the system one at a time, thereby meeting the criteria of reducing risk and minimizing interruption of daily hospital operations.
4. Introducing the most cost-effective features of the system early will assure most support from the controller.
5. Risk is reduced, because several of the functions of the system can be isolated. A breakdown in one area will not debilitate the entire computer system.

A. Personnel

During the last reporting period we noted that the development of the proposed system will require a substantial number of personnel. When the system is operational, however, most of the additional people will not be needed anymore. Therefore, the hospital will contract with an outside computer service company to

III. Conclusion

design, develop, and implement the system. To meet the maintenance and operating requirements, however, the hospital will have to do the staffing. Although some control will be lost and some uncertainties assumed by relying on outside support, this approach has the following benefits:

1. The hospital staff will not be burdened with searching for, hiring, training, and later releasing the development staff.
2. An agreement for the development and implementation of the system can be entered into at a fixed price.
3. The contract can state that beyond a specific date the service company must pay a certain fine if the project is not completed (i.e., the system is not up and running). Thus the risk that the project will fall behind schedule is minimized.
4. Since the hospital's data processing staff is not engaged in the detail design, programming, and testing, they will have the time to learn the total system and develop their maintenance expertise.

B. Equipment

Our study shows that many of the functions performed by the total system are related, and in some cases interlocking. Since data transferral may be needed between files and for reports that include information from more than one functional area, the team is considering the use of a single, mainframe computer as opposed to decentralized mini or micro processors. Although more work will be done in this area, this option appears to offer the following benefits:

1. Allows communication between individual programs and files.
2. Retains capability to increase integration in the future.
3. Centralizes data processing activities, which promotes better organization, increases efficiency, and controls data management.
4. Provides more main memory for future larger systems.
5. Allows multiprogramming, which makes better use of machine time.

III. CONCLUSION

Our projected activities to be performed by the next reporting period (November 3, 1981) are:

1. Review the applications identified and expand the detailed requirements.
2. Evaluate the hardware requirements of the applications.
3. Generate specific hardware requirements for the total system.
4. Review conclusions and their justifications with key hospital personnel.
5. Draft the RFP.

Chapter Seven
Writing Usable Procedures

Accurate, functional written procedures that are kept current by periodic updating are essential communication tools in every phase of data processing. In fact, for uniformity and efficiency; for ease of learning and understanding whatever type of work the new or transferred employee is assigned to do, written standardized procedures are absolutely necessary. Procedures, very much like application programs, cannot be written without a thorough knowledge of the specific applications' requirements and functions, and the expected results. Simply put, procedures—which are definitive, clearly written, step by step instructions enabling employees to perform a specific task(s)—have to be tailor-made.

Specifically, the level of technology presented, the language, the style, and the format of the procedures must be geared to a particular audience. (Defining your audience is discussed in Part I, Chapter 3.) This is true whether the written procedures are for defining a system or program specifications, preparing data for computer input, manually producing a product, or providing a service to the company.

Moreover, the key word in any procedure is *suitability*. For example, though both programmers and computer operators (technicians, if you will), work with programs, they need very different written procedures to help them perform their jobs.

Ideally, all DP facilities in this country would use the same standards for written procedures. In the real world, however, because no two enterprises—not even in the same field—operate in the same manner, this is quite impossible.

Consequently, it is a decision by middle management as to which type, format, and style of procedure among the many accepted procedures format is to be standardized for the particular activity, for the particular facility. Once the decision is made, it is imperative that the selected type of standard procedures is established and *enforced*.

In addition to HIPO and SADT procedures (mostly used for system design and development, as detailed in the previous chapter), there is an array of various types of standard procedures.

Before describing and illustrating with sample applications the most widely used procedure types, perhaps a discussion of what the process of writing procedures consists of is in order. It is made up of the following steps:

1. Preliminary steps/considerations.
2. Final copy.
3. Follow-up/updating method.
4. Sign-off/approval.

1. PRELIMINARY STEPS/CONSIDERATIONS

Since today the majority of companies have written procedures for most activities, usually it's only for new activities that you have to develop procedures "from scratch." If these new activities are generated because a new system is being designed, developed, and implemented, then the procedures, to be effective, should be developed concurrent with the DP project.

In all cases, however, you must know what is the nature of the task(s); what is the most efficient way of doing it; and what are the precise steps to accomplish the task(s). You also must know the proper sequence or flow of work of the task(s). (See Figure 9, sample work flowchart, Part One, Chapter 5.) And you must measure each written procedure against the criteria: is it well organized? is it functional? is it easy to follow? and is it easy to reference? To achieve these criteria, you have to:

1. Study existing documentation about the particular activity or process to determine whether it can be updated or improved, or whether the procedures described are obsolete and new ones are needed. In case of a system being developed, make sure to get from the project leader and/or systems designer all the data and information about the procedures involved in the DP project.

Preliminary Steps/Considerations

VERIFY EACH ACTIVITY

2. Observe at first hand the activity to be documented and standardized. Take notes of every step the employee takes to perform his/her task(s). In addition, either before or after, interview and tape record the employee's supervisor about the specific activity.

Of course, you need the permission of the supervisor to observe how the experienced employee(s) is executing the task(s), *and* the permission of the department manager to interview the supervisor. The latter permission is obviously unnecessary if it is the department head who asked you to improve, update, or write new procedures.

CHECK SOFTWARE BY USING IT

NOTE: When you have finished taking notes and completed your interview(s), it is essential to use the software to check the accuracy and completeness of what you observed and what you were told. Of course, if you are writing original procedures simultaneously with the development of a new project, there may be no software to use at this point, and you will have to postpone this activity.

3. After your notes are typed (or better yet keyed in to a word-processing system), and your interview(s) transcribed, show the rough draft to the employee whose work you studied at first hand, and to the employee's supervisor whom you interviewed.

HANDLE DISCREPANCIES DIPLOMATICALLY

At times you will find that the supervisor's version of procedures differs from what his/her subordinate does. Indeed, it is not uncommon that a supervisor thinks a procedure is being performed one way, when in fact it is being performed differently.

In such cases you must be diplomatic. Show the subordinate's version to the supervisor, and ask if it meets his or her approval. Do not mention the discrepancy between the descriptions.

4. If there are established documentation standards for written procedures, follow them by all means. However, if they are poorly written or out of date, or if no standards

for written procedures exist, bring this to the attention of the department manager. The probabilities are that the department manager will ask you to define and establish quality documentation standards for procedures.

A NOTE OF CAUTION: Unless you establish the standards *cooperatively* with the staff who will be using it, you will run into problems. By involving the staff, you ensure that they will be comfortable with your written procedures and use them.

MATCH LEVEL OF TECHNICAL INFORMATION WITH THE AUDIENCE

5. Choose the language, style, format, and most important, the level of technical information that are appropriate for the defined audience.

ASK FOR READERS' COMMENTS ON YOUR DRAFT

6. When your second draft is finished, make enough copies so that the department manager as well as the supervisor and employees involved in that particular activity can have one. Don't forget to include a cover memorandum requesting the readers to write their comments, suggestions, and criticisms directly on the copy. The memorandum, because it's dated, is insurance for you against possible future criticism if, on account of a tardy response from one of the reviewers, you cannot meet your target date, or if a person claims a month later that he/she didn't see the procedures until "this morning."

RESUBMIT YOUR DRAFT TO THE SAME PARTIES

7. The third draft, which must reflect consideration of the suggestions received as well as correction of the criticized points, should be submitted again to the same parties, and again with a cover memorandum. Generally, three or at the most four drafts are sufficient. Then, except perhaps for a few minor changes, the material is ready to be produced as the final copy.

NOTE: While waiting for critiques for the third draft, confer with the draftsman or technical illustrator (if there's one) to ensure that, when you are ready to hand to management the finished procedures, all the tables, charts, and exhibits are ready too.

A GLOSSARY CAN BE VERY HELPFUL TO USERS OF PROCEDURES

2. FINAL COPY

After proofreading the final copy of your procedures, which according to your last feedback are correct and satisfactory, add the table of contents, and if appropriate a glossary to define the acronyms or initials that are in the procedures. You may also want to add words that are unique to the industry or field that your DP facility is part of. The latter can be a great help to new employees who are not familiar with the particular industry's "language."

3. FOLLOW-UP/UPDATING METHOD

Unless the firm is very small, the procedures writer is not responsible for such physical follow-ups as keeping track of how many copies are printed, or distributing the manuals. However, the writer is responsible for providing a method—the simpler the better—to keep the procedures manual(s) current. Generally, an "UPDATING LOG" form placed right after the title page and before the table of contents will satisfy that requirement. Thus, when the department manager signs off (see Section 4 below), he/she approves not only your written procedures but the updating/follow-up method as well. A sample updating log form follows.

SAMPLE Updating Log

INSTRUCTION:
Whenever any updates or changes occur in these procedures, new pages will be issued. Please update the manual by removing the obsolete page and replacing it with the new page. Also, to keep track of the updates, enter the date received and the new page number in line with each Update Number. Bulletins are to be handled the same way as update or change pages.

UPDATE #	DATE	PAGE #	UPDATE #	DATE	PAGE #
1			21		
2			22		
3			23		
4			24		
5			25		
6			26		
7			27		
8			28		
9			29		
10			30		
11			31		
12			32		
13			33		
14			34		
15			35		
16			36		
17			37		
18			38		
19			39		
20			40		

4. SIGN-OFF/APPROVAL

As a final but very important step before the procedures are duplicated and distributed, get the written approval of the department manager. This ensures you against any possible future problems.

To make the sign-off as easy as possible for the manager, at the bottom of the title page add the word "APPROVED," the "Date _____," the manager's name, and space for his/her signature.

And now to acquaint you with the standard procedures formats in this country. The following are the four most widely used formats:

1. Text pattern.
2. Text-flowchart pattern.
3. Picture pattern.
4. Playscript pattern.

TEXT FORMAT IS THE TRADITIONAL TYPE OF PROCEDURES

1. **The text pattern** is the traditional procedures format. For a simple procedure such as the following sample application "A," the text pattern is well-suited. Because it is straight narrative, this format is favored by unsophisticated technical or administrative writers as the easiest type of procedures format to write. Text type of procedures, however, are difficult to reference, especially when they are describing a lengthy task. Also, the text pattern procedures tend to be dull reading, unless the writer makes a special effort to make the text easy to read if not interesting.

Programming procedures, though not strictly "straight text," belong in this category. These procedures or instructions are used by programmers whenever they need to know *what* is the function of a certain program, and *how* to use a particular program. (See the following sample applications B(1) and B(2).)

Finally, user guides/procedures, though often extensively illustrated, belong in this category also. These procedures provide instructions to DP and non-DP users on how to use a particular computer system (on-line and often in real time) as part of their jobs. Because the great majority of user guides are written for non-DP people, the following sample application "C" is an example of such document.

SAMPLE **Application A**

SYSTEMS DEPARTMENT
STANDARD OPERATING PROCEDURES

Div.
Dept.
Date
Author

TITLE: MAIL ROOM PROCEDURES

1. Pick up mail at 8:30 a.m. at the post office.
2. Stamp today's date on all mail.
3. Open and sort registered mail.
4. Sort other mail by color code and post office box number.
5. Route corporate correspondence (P.O. box #500) UNOPENED to the internal courier.
6. Open all other mail.
7. Attach an internal control card (Form #2461) to each envelope.
8. Place the sorted, open mail in designated postal trays according to color code and P.O. box number.
9. Take the full postal trays to the extraction section.
10. Remove mail from the trays and place them in the machine hopper.
11. Activate the Automatic Mail Extractor and the auto-feed function.
12. When the machine completes its function, place all postal trays with the extracted mail on the mobile cart.
13. Deliver the mail to the appropriate departments.

SAMPLE Application B(1)

JONAS INC.

DATA PROCESSING CENTER

Project/Program Name		Project No. Date
Procedure Name	ASMFC	Program No.

ASMFC is a standard IBM procedure for assembling programs. The following is an example of using the procedure:

```
//jobname    JOB    Acct. info., programmer, Class-C
//step       EXEC   ASMFC
//SM.SYSIN   DD     Source deck data set
//
```

SAMPLE Application B(2)

JONAS INC.

DATA PROCESSING CENTER

Project/Program Name		Project No. Date
Procedure Name	COBUCLG	Program No.

COBUCLG provides the capability to compile, link-edit, and test COBOL programs. This procedure should be performed while testing a new version of a program, without doing a permanent link-edit.

The following is an example of using the procedure:

```
//jobname    JOB    Acct. info., programmer, Class-B
//step       EXEC   COBUCLG
//COB.SYSIN  DD     Input source desk
//GO.FILEX   DD     Go step data sets
//
```

SAMPLE Application C

I. BETANET SYSTEM

Betanet is a national computerized information network designed specifically for the real estate market. It carries information on real estate transactions throughout the country by state and region, as well as all the additional information that is vital to a broker.

The computer network, designed and operated by Betanet, Inc., Albany, NY, provides timely data to increase the sales of its subscribers. Moreover, the procedures for using Betanet can be learned in a short time by following the simple instructions in this manual. You will be able to use Betanet via your display terminal productively within a couple of days, if not within your first day.

A. Your Display Terminal

Your terminal, consisting of a keyboard and display screen, is the tool that allows you to access information on the Betanet System. However, before any keyed (typed) message can be relayed by telephone from your terminal into the computer in New York, it has to go through an electronic device called a "modem." Because computer terminals and computers have one language, and the telephone another, the modem is needed to translate from one to the other. In short, it is the modem that allows the terminal and the computer to converse with each other through the telephone lines.

B. The Keyboard

To get the most out of your display terminal, you should know that in addition to the regular typewriter keys it has extra keys that are important to the various system functions.

Your attention is called to one key: RETURN (carriage return). You will use this key more often than any other key because you have to press it whenever you are sending information to the computer, whenever you are inquiring about some data, or whenever you are ordering the system to retrieve specific information for you.

C. Your "User Identification" and Password

Because the data you key in might be confidential, it has to be safeguarded. Accordingly, an identification (ID) will be assigned to you made up of two numbers followed by two letters, for example, 37RA, *and* a unique "password" consisting of three numbers and three letters, for example, 372RAH. Without the proper user ID and password, nobody is able to "sign-on" to the system to get information; in fact, nobody is even able to hook up with the computer.

D. The "Sign-On" Procedure

1. Press the ATTN key on your terminal.
2. The computer system will respond with: "ENTER ID" on your video screen.
3. Type your user ID, and press the RETURN key.
4. The system will respond with: "ENTER PASSWORD."
5. Type your password and press the RETURN key.
6. The system will respond with: "READY," indicating that you can enter your command to request or send information, or just to review certain data that is stored in the computer.

E. The "Sign-Off" Procedure

1. Type "BYE" and press the RETURN key to tell the computer that you are through with using the system today or at this particular time.
2. The system will respond with: "SIGNED OFF at 11:53, Mar. 19, 1982 (The hour, minute, month, day, year).

TEXT-FLOWCHART FORMAT IS AN OFTEN USED PROCEDURES TYPE

2. The text-flowchart pattern, a combination of the text and flowchart types of procedures, offers certain advantages over both the text and the flowchart formats. It is visual, it provides written instructions that complement the flowchart, and you can reference any step because of the number scheme that ties each flowchart symbol to a specific written instruction. Moreover, the flowchart that winds through the left side of all pages illustrating the particular procedures breaks the monotony of the text, thus making it easier for a new or transferred employee to learn the procedures.

For consistency and better understanding of the various formats, the same "Mail Room Procedures" (Figure 23) are used in the following sample application "D" as were used in sample application "A."

Procedures for computer operators fall into this category too. These procedures may be called "Computer Opera-

Sign-Off/Approval

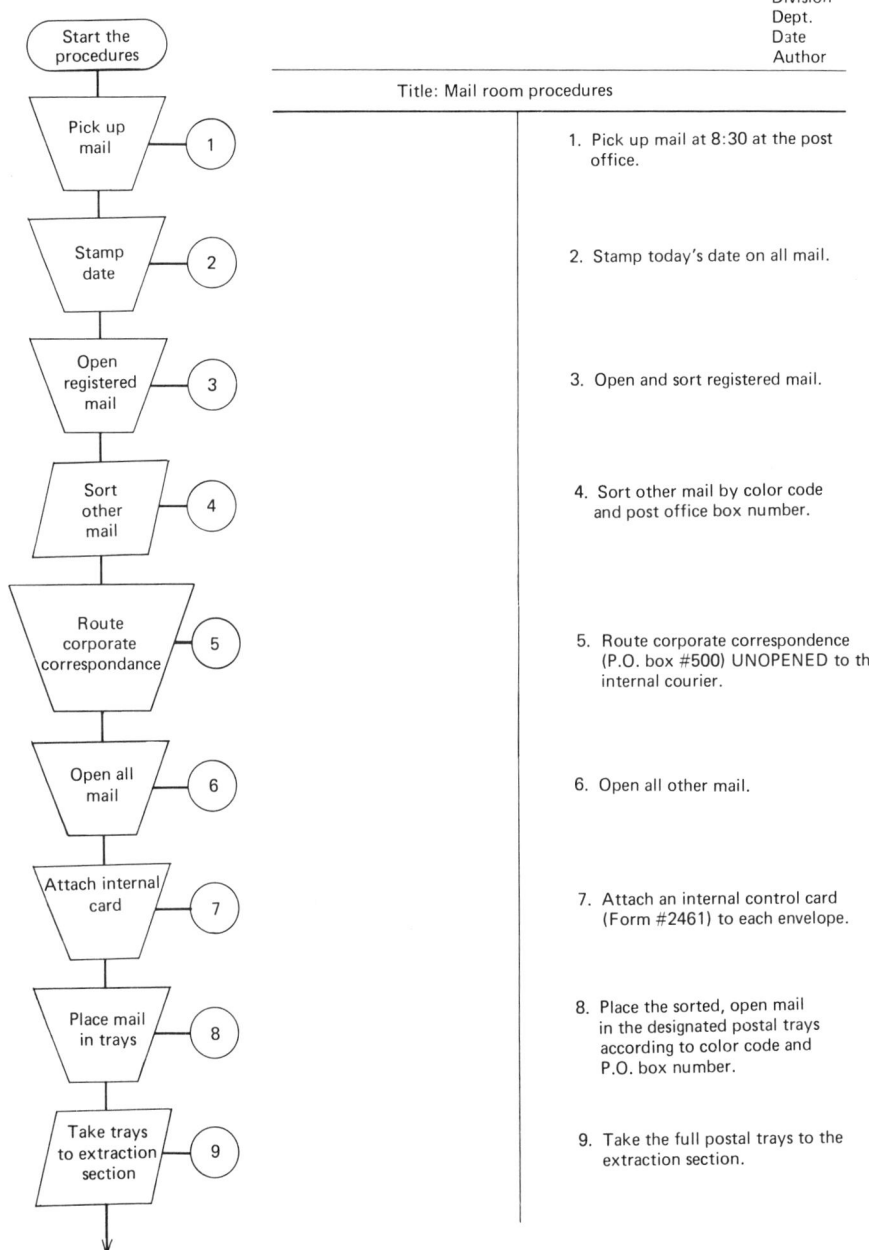

Figure 23. Sample application D: Systems department standard operating procedures. Mail room procedures.

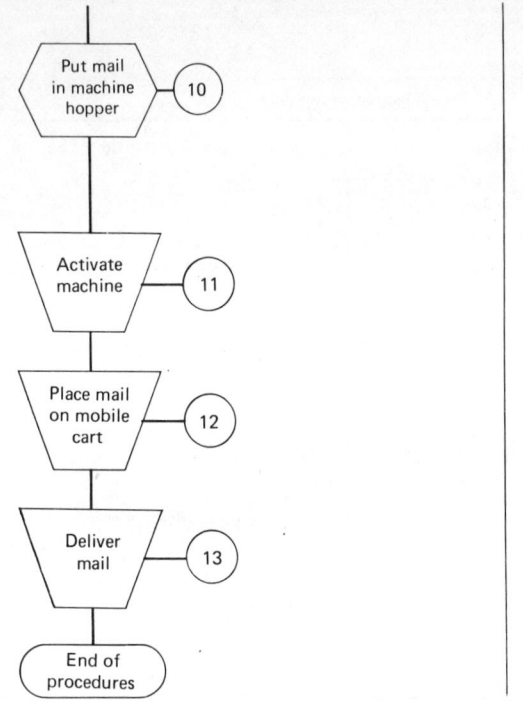

Figure 23. Continued.

tions Manual," or more often than not they are called "Runbook." Because computer operators run jobs (each job may contain one or more programs) and not programs, there must be a runbook for each application, or system, or subsystem. Moreover, a runbook, at minimum, *must* have a job step/job stream flowchart that shows clearly labeled input files and cards (if any), processing programs, and output files and reports that the programs generate, as well as the disposition of these outputs. The following sample application "E" (Figure 24) consists of several pages of a customary runbook combining text and flowcharts.

SAMPLE Application E

JONAS INC.

DATA PROCESSING CENTER

Procedure title	Accounts Receivable (A/R) Procedures	Procedure Number ARP 50	Prepared by
Checked by		Approved by	Date prepared

JOB STEP/JOB STREAM FLOWCHART

Job name: ACR0001 Procedure name: AR1020DY Frequency: Daily
Program name: A/R Transaction listing Approximate running time: 10 minutes

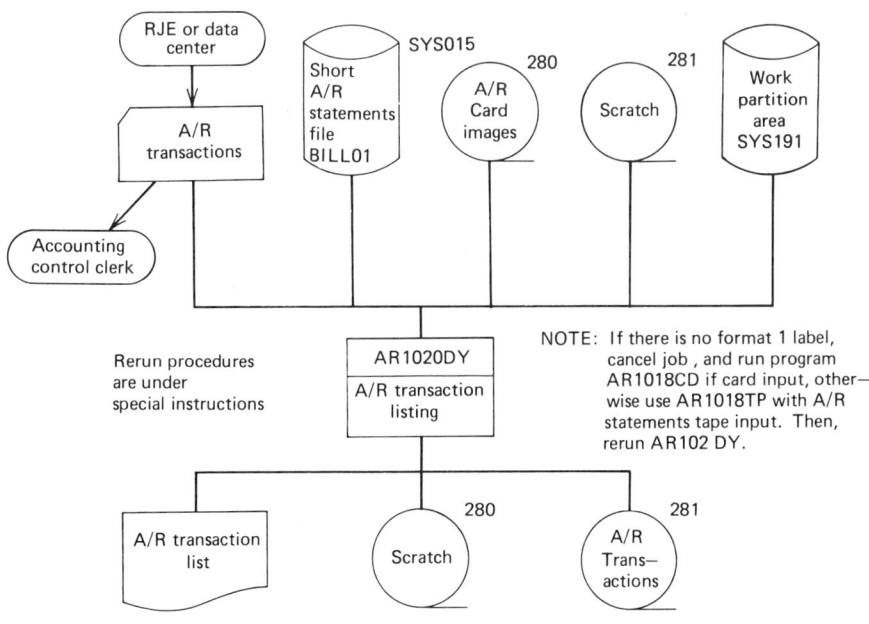

NOTE: The branches send a message via RJE, requesting A/R transactions for specific branches and dates. The Data Center then loads these cards to tape, using / / job load. This tape is then input to AR1020DY, which is executed from the branches via RJE.

Figure 24. Sample application E: Job step/job stream flowchart.

117

SPECIAL INSTRUCTIONS

Job name: ACR0001   Procedure name: AR1020DY

Send message to the Data Center *at least 30 minutes prior* to the time that AR1020DY is run. The message should tell the Data Center what branch number(s) and what date is to run.

The reason for the extra time is to give the Data Center enough time to load the A/R transactions for that specific date to a tape. When this run is completed, it creates an A/R transaction tape at the Data Center.

Rerun Procedures

There are 3 reasons why this job may blow up: 1. bad input tape: 2. data exception; 3. cards left out, either by the branches or the Data Center.

1. **Bad input tape.** Recreate the input tape, reload the cards to a new tape, and rerun the job.
2. **Data exception.** Check the Data Center's input cards, and if necessary the branches' input cards (the error is either triple punch or blank cards). Pull out the bad cards, insert the correct ones, and rerun the job.
3. **Cards left out.** Scratch output tape, reload the input cards PLUS the missing data. Back out to the input tape, and rerun the job. That is, if the cards were left out at the *Data Center.*

    If the cards were left out at the RJE terminal of a branch or branches, they have to reload the input cards PLUS the missing data, and rerun, that is, resubmit the cards via RJE.

ERROR MESSAGES

Job name: ACR0001	Procedure name: AR1020DY
Console message	Action
"TAPE INPUT Y YES, N NO"	Self-explanatory
"ANSWER CORRECT Y YES N NO"	Self-explanatory

"ENTER BR NO XXXXXXXXXX"	Enter branch number:
	   1 Albany
	   3 Long Island
	   4 Brooklyn
	   5 Ithaca

Sign-Off/Approval

	6 Elmira
	8 Bronx
	9 Warehouse
"CE OR T CARDS NOT FIRST CARDS IN ACCT"	No action is necessary

PICTURE FORMAT IS A PROCEDURES TYPE PREFERRED BY ENGINEERS

3. **The picture pattern** is favored by engineering and construction firms because of its terse and uncomplicated format. This procedures format, however, is equally well-suited for administrative or clerical tasks, as sample application "F" (Figure 25) (using the "Mail Room Procedures" again) proves it.

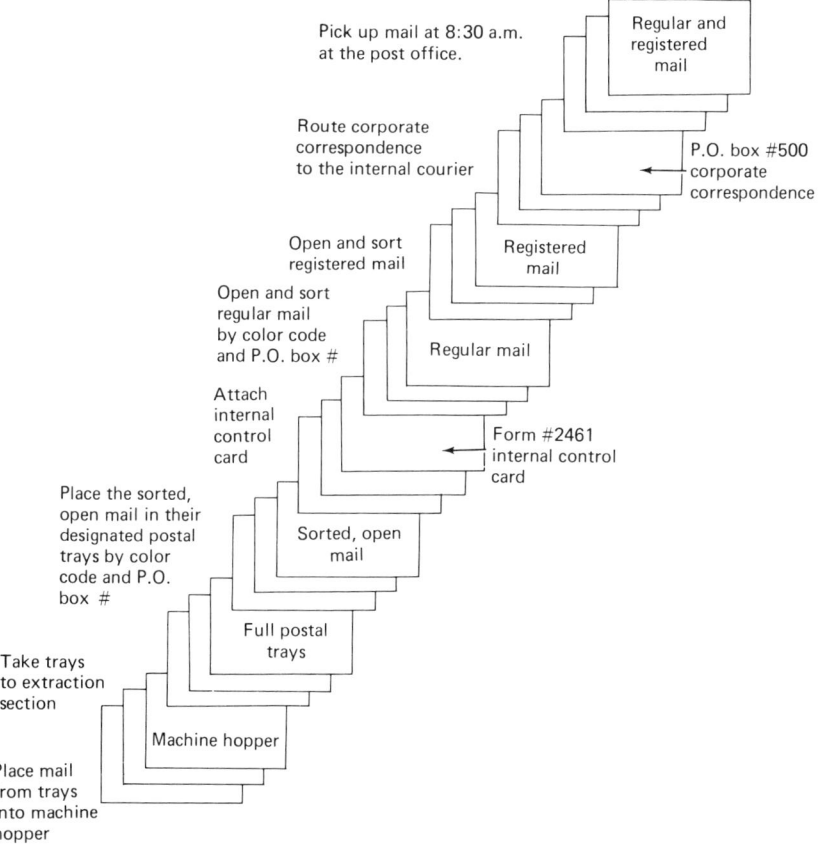

Figure 25. Sample application F: Systems department standard operating procedures. Mail room procedures.

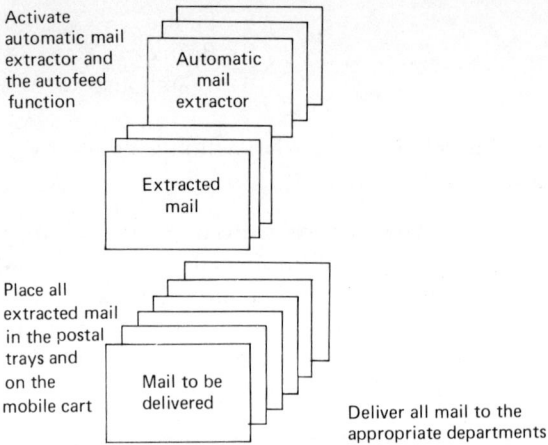

Figure 25. Continued.

PLAYSCRIPT FORMAT IS THE MOST POPULAR PROCEDURES TYPE

4. **The playscript pattern** is the most popular type of procedures format for manual or computer-related functions because the clerk, technician, operator, and so on, can easily follow each step to perform definitive tasks. Moreover, a "NOTE" (or several of them) can be inserted in the left column without interrupting the flow of instructions in the right column. A "NOTE" can caution the employee about a possible pitfall in the task, it can tell the employee where in the scheme of operations his/her specific task(s) fits in, and so forth. And that is one of the reasons why "playscripting" is favored in so many enterprises.

The pages in playscript type of procedures are divided into two columns just as in the text-flowchart pattern. The left column, under the heading of "TASK," lists the task and the form(s) to be used with the specific task(s) by name and number. The right column, under the heading of "ACTIVITY," provides a step-by-step *functional* description of each action. Sample Application "G" that follows shows how the by-now familiar "Mail Room Procedures" can be presented in this format.

SAMPLE **Application G**

SYSTEMS DEPARTMENT
STANDARD OPERATING PROCEDURES

	Div.
	Dept.
	Date
	Author

TITLE: MAIL ROOM PROCEDURES

Task	Activity
Processing the mail	

Processing the mail
Control form: Internal Control Card, number 2461

NOTE: Color code indicates the different processing that particular mail will go through; the P.O. box number indicates the particular department where the matter will be taken care of.

1. Pick up mail at 8:30 at the post office.
2. Stamp today's date on all mail.
3. Open and sort registered mail.
4. Sort other mail by color code and post office box number.
5. Route corporate correspondence (P.O. box #500) UNOPENED to the internal courier.
6. Open all other mail.
7. Attach an internal control card (Form #2461) to each envelope.
8. Place the sorted, open mail in designated postal trays according to color code and P.O. box number.
9. Take the full postal trays to the extraction section.
10. Remove mail from the trays and place them in the machine hopper.
11. Activate the Automatic Mail Extractor and the auto-feed function.

12. When the machine completes its function, place all postal trays with the extracted mail on the mobile cart.
13. Deliver the mail to the appropriate departments.

Chapter Eight
Writing the Systems Study

A great variety of studies, from the feasibility study and operations study to functional specifications and design specifications,* are labeled "systems studies." The type of systems study, however, that DP professionals are most frequently asked to do (unless they are systems designers) is the feasibility study.

Since many DP professionals have never written this particular study until they are called upon to undertake such a project, perhaps a definition of it is in order. A feasibility study is the result of an in-depth investigation and analysis of all relevant data and factors, and the subsequent definition of the particular problem(s), proposed project, or idea. It reviews valid alternatives and recommends a technically feasible and cost-beneficial solution, taking into consideration an essential component: the human factor.

There are two types of feasibility study: (1) for a particular department(s), and (2) for an entire organization.

1. This type of feasibility study includes, for example, a study on the practicality of a proposed new or modified forecasting system for the sales department, or a new/restructured inventory control system to supply information to the warehouse, the order department, and the purchase department.

2. This type of feasibility study involves, for example, a study on the practicality of an entire firm's contemplated conversion from a file management system to a data base management system (DBMS), or a conversion from a centralized data base to distributed data bases. Because of its scope and complexity, obviously this study involves much more time and effort than the first type of feasibility study.

---

*A brief sample of design specifications is provided at the end of this chapter.

Before starting on a feasibility study project, make sure that your assignment, whether from the top corporate executive or from the manager of a particular department, is in writing, preferably in a formal manner.

You must be aware, however, that it is a rare written assignment that defines clearly and precisely the problems (reasons for needing the study) and the objectives (desired results). In most cases the stated problems are only symptomatic, and the objectives idealistic. Consequently, more often than not it is up to you to ferret out the real problems and define realistic objectives.

To accomplish your assignment in an organized and professional manner, you should:

1. Plan your course of action.
2. Investigate and define the problem(s) or the proposed project.
3. Identify the constraints.
4. Research and analyze possible solutions as they apply to specific problems.
5. Develop a solution that will meet the objectives within the matrix of existing constraints.

1. PLANNING THE FEASIBILITY STUDY PROJECT

To establish the direction of the study and to ensure that no important steps are left out, you should plan your course of action, using the written assignment as a general guide.

ESTABLISH TENTATIVE OBJECTIVES, SCOPE, AND SCHEDULE

The mechanics of your plan, while comprised of most phases discussed in Chapter 4, "Steps Prior To Writing," will differ somewhat because, as already noted, you may not have *clearly defined* objectives at this early juncture. However, using the assignment, you should be able to tentatively determine the objectives, scope, and schedule for your project.

Developing a Solution

BEST DATA GATHERING TOOL: INTERVIEWS

2. INVESTIGATING AND DEFINING THE PROBLEMS

Although much of the data necessary to define the problems may be gathered by researching written materials—what there might be, how to find it, where to find it, and so on—the primary investigating tool, as in all types of systems study, is the interview.

You have to talk to all the people involved in the current operations and/or procedures. (Effective interviewing techniques are discussed in detail in Chapter 4, "Steps Prior to Writing.")

When the interviewing is complete, you should be able to define the real problems, thus confirming, clarifying, or redefining the problems stated in the written assignment.

WATCH OUT FOR CONSTRAINTS

3. IDENTIFYING EXISTING CONSTRAINTS

It is very important to identify existing constraints when considering new, modified, or restructured systems, since they could affect the recommended system's reliability and cost-effectiveness.

LOOK INTO ALL POSSIBLE ALTERNATIVES

4. RESEARCHING AND ANALYZING POSSIBLE ALTERNATIVES

Because not only equipment and software have to be considered but various processes as well (as they apply in toto to the defined problems), this phase usually involves a great amount of research, effort, and time.

YOUR SOLUTION SHOULD MEET MANAGEMENT OBJECTIVES AND STAFF REQUIREMENTS

5. DEVELOPING A SOLUTION

At the end of the "alternatives" phase, you should be able to develop a solution that will meet the established objectives within the existing constraints. Before you recommend a particular solution in writing, however, you should verify each aspect of the system. Specifically, its cost, technical operations required, operating procedures, effectiveness, benefits for the organization (taking into account the requirements of employees who would be involved in the operation of the recommended system), equipment necessary to support the system's functions, and implementation.

Since visual displays enhance a presentation, you should have at minimum a flowchart of the logical processes and their sequence, and a physical data flow diagram. Further, no feasibility study is complete without a table of the estimated costs for the recommended system, preferably on a separate page.

Last but certainly not least, you should discuss two issues that are of growing concern to management: security and control. Within these two important areas you should consider: physical security; data security (how to guard against intentional or unintentional unauthorized accessing of unique files and data in the system); logical control; data accuracy; and system security. And, if appropriate (as in the case of a bank system, health care system, hospital system, etc.), you should discuss privacy, that is, how you intend to protect confidential information about customers/clients.

6. WRITING THE FEASIBILITY STUDY

If you have planned your project carefully, gathered data systematically, defined the problems, objectives, and constraints accurately, researched and analyzed the various alternatives, and developed a solution that will meet the objectives, then the writing of the study is a relatively easy task. You may have to go through a couple of drafts before you are satisfied with the material, but the task should consist mainly of editing your notes into a lucid and concise yet comprehensive report.

Packaging, as noted throughout this book, is important. Your carefully written feasibility study deserves as attractive a format and package as possible. Consequently, if the paper is longer than six pages, it should be in a binder, preferably one with a transparent plastic cover.

Writing the Feasibility Study

And the layout format should make for easy reading and easy referencing. Specifically, it should have wide margins, double-spaced text, and many headings.

COMPONENTS OF THE FEASIBILITY REPORT

The format of the feasibility study should consist of some or all of the following components:

a. **Title page.** The title should be descriptive but compact. Five or six spaces under the title the date should appear. Still further down your name and title should be stated. And last, the name of the company, and the name of the department if applicable, should appear.

b. **Table of contents.** Unless the study is only five or six pages long, list the main sections and headings here, as well as any charts, tables, and other exhibits.

c. **Summary/abstract.** This should be clear and succinct, designed for the executive who wants to review the problems and get the gist of your recommended solution without having to read the complete paper.

d. **Objectives.** This section lists tersely the objectives that the recommended system must meet.

e. **Introduction/background.** This section should be brief, not more than two or three short paragraphs. It should give a concise overview of the enterprise (if the study involves the entire organization), or of the department (if the study concerns a particular department), its data processing capabilities, and its functions, if appropriate.

f. **Statement of the problem.** This section should be on a separate page, especially when the project is large and complex. Here, drawing on the written assignment and on your investigation, describe the problem(s) encountered by the company or department.

g. **Identification of constraints.** This section states the constraints you had to take into consideration in recommending the solution.

h. **Technical discussion.** This is the main body of the feasibility study. It gives in detail the "what," "how," and "why" of your recommended solution. It lists the equipment and software required, and describes the proper implementation method.

i. **Security and control.** This section is becoming an extremely important part of the feasibility study. Consequently, the recommendations in it should be comprehensive yet cost-effective.

j. **Cost analysis.** This is a decisive section of the feasibility study, and should be on a separate page for ease of reference by management and the controller. Cost analysis includes not only the estimated costs for the system, but the estimated benefits as well. In fact, unless there are qualitative benefits that answer management objectives, usually the project is canceled because it would not be feasible to continue it.

A sample feasibility study on a complex project affecting a whole enterprise follows. So that the reader can use the example as a practical model, the presented material is not an abbreviated version: *it is a complete report*.

This is followed by a brief sample of another, different type of systems study (as noted in the footnote on the first page of this chapter): *design specifications*.

SAMPLE Feasibility Study on the Development of a Distributed Data Processing System

September 12, 1981

STEREO MANUFACTURING COMPANY
Sacramento, California

Michael F. Meagher
Senior Business Systems Analyst

CONTENTS

Section	Page
I. SUMMARY	131
II. OBJECTIVES	131
III. BACKGROUND	132
IV. STATEMENT OF THE PROBLEM	132
V. IDENTIFICATION OF CONSTRAINTS	133
VI. TECHNICAL DISCUSSION	133
1. Sales Schedules	133
2. Production Schedule	133
3. Material Ordering Schedule	133
4. Potential Overages/Shortages	134
5. Operating Procedures	134
VII. EQUIPMENT	134
VIII. IMPLEMENTATION	136
IX. SECURITY AND CONTROL	138
X. COST ANALYSIS	140

LIST OF ILLUSTRATIONS

Figures

Logical Processes Flowchart of the Proposed System	135
Hardware Configurations and Physical Data Flow of the Proposed System	137
Implementation Time Table of the Proposed System	138

I. SUMMARY

This feasibility study presents a possible solution to the Company's current problems concerning lack of timely and too often unreliable information for use by sales, production, and purchasing management. The existing leased IBM 370/155 is unsatisfactory both as to cost-effectiveness and to serving the data processing needs of the Company. Consequently, I recommend replacing the IBM 370/155 with a cost-beneficial centralized data processing network,* using IBM 4331 as the central processor unit. Though 4331 is a minicomputer, it is compatible with the 370/155, and consequently, the Accounts Receivable and Payroll/Personnel systems—the only two applications automated and on the large mainframe—will need but minor program modifications to be run on the 4331.

This centralized network approach would provide the Company timely and accurate information as well as substantial savings over the costly large mainframe now being used. The IBM 4331, being a minicomputer, doesn't require the expensive air conditioning, can be leased for much less than IBM 370/155, and doesn't need the large space that a mainframe must have. Moreover, each sales location would be able to retrieve and send information on-line in real-time to the central data base.

II. OBJECTIVES

Following is a list of objectives that the proposed system must meet.

1. The system must be able to accurately predict the number of completed units available for sale on any given date for the next 12 months for each sales office.
2. The system must provide the information that the units available on a given day have been committed. This must be available to all sales offices so that the same units are not recommitted.

---

*A centralized network is one in which several computers (usually microcomputers) are at different geographical locations and interact with the central facility (usually a minicomputer), which contains all the data bases and possibly all application programs.

3. The system must provide the Production Department with the sales schedules for a 1-year period, so that production can be planned.
4. The system must provide the Purchasing Department with up-to-date inventory (raw materials, subassemblies, and finished products) and production schedules, so that materials in short supply can be procured before they run out, delaying production.
5. The system must provide each production manager in each factory with information as to what raw materials and subassemblies will be reaching his or her plant each day, so that each day's production schedule can be modified as necessary.
6. Through the system it must be possible to interactively modify sales and production schedules up to a predetermined time. After this specified time there can be no changes in sales or production schedules for a given day.
7. The system must be capable of maintaining actual sales records for each sales location and for the Company as a whole, on an up-to-the-minute basis.

III. BACKGROUND

Stereo Manufacturing Company's current nationwide network of 50 sales offices are responsible for the wholesale marketing of the SMC products. The corporate headquarters is located close to the Company's only warehouse, and to the three factories where the products are assembled in stages.

Data processing capabilities are provided by an in-house (leased) IBM 370/155. The only functions that are automated at the present time are the Accounts Receivable and the Payroll/Personnel.

IV. STATEMENT OF THE PROBLEM

The Company faces the following problems:

1. Requests to the warehouse for inventory information on raw materials, subcomponents, and finished units must be in writing. A response, however, usually takes three days.
2. The managers at each factory do not know when components or subassemblies will arrive; thus production schedules cannot be prepared until the materials are actually delivered. This causes inefficient operations and a certain amount of idle time.
3. The remote sales offices, which have no information on finished unit inventories or production schedules, are making commitments to delivery dates

that cannot be met. The above are obviously more than just inventory problems. Sales and production scheduling also need to be considered.

V. IDENTIFICATION OF CONSTRAINTS

The following constraints exist and have been taken into consideration in analyzing alternatives and recommending a solution.

1. A budget of $180,000 for system development of this project has been recently determined.
2. Management requires the system to be implemented in 10 months. This tight schedule may cause poor implementation and inadequate user training.
3. The Company has no trained personnel with data processing network concepts. This factor may affect system reliability.
4. Each sales office is independent of all others.

These constraints will need to be reviewed periodically by management to increase the system's cost effectiveness.

VI. TECHNICAL DISCUSSION

The system I recommend to replace the IBM 370/155 and meet the stated objectives is a combination of manual and automated processes, in the beginning anyway. A description of these processes and the responsibilities for performing them follows.

1. **Sales Schedules.** Sales schedule for each of the 50 sales locations is to be prepared by the respective regional sales manager. These schedules are to be produced manually, probably on an incremental basis over the previous year's schedules. When complete, the detail for each location is to be entered in the computer, which then generates a Company Summary report.
2. **Production Schedule.** Concurrent to the production of the Company Summary, a Production Schedule report and an Exception Report are generated by the computer system. The Exception Report is to identify for the regional sales managers areas in which sales will be at a level that will strain or exceed production capabilities.
3. **Material Ordering Schedule.** Once the production schedule is established, a material ordering schedule can be prepared to improve the timely flow of raw materials to the factories. As soon as the details on average length of time

required to receive each type of material is known, a computer application is to be developed to produce the basic material ordering schedule as a guide to the Purchasing Department.
4. **Potential Overages/Shortages.** The details of sales and production activities must be entered immediately into the system by respective sales field offices and departments. This is to ensure that potential overages or shortages of finished goods inventories are projected. Exception reports of potential overages and shortages are to be produced for management as input for corporate decision making.
5. **Operating Procedures.** Upon receiving an order from a customer, the salesperson enters into the video display terminal (VDT) (each sales location is to have at least one VDT) details of the transaction: product code, number of units, customer name and address (or customer code, if the order is given by an existing customer), unit price quoted, and shipping date. When these data are input, the system performs a number of functions such as editing for valid product code and customer code, checking the unit price to make sure it falls within accepted ranges, changing the file containing units available by date to reduce the units available on the committed shipping date.

A new file is established, containing details of the order to be transmitted to other computer applications that produce shipping orders, invoices, computations of commissions for sales persons, and Accounts Receivable input.

A flowchart displaying the logical process is shown in Figure 26.

VII. EQUIPMENT

To implement the recommended system I suggest the following equipment:

1. An IBM 4331 central processing unit (the minicomputer that is to contain the data bases) with appropriate peripheral devices.
2. A microprocessor at each regional sales headquarters to handle communications processing and multiplexing functions.
3. Communications processors* at the high-volume sales sites that have 10 or more video display terminals to justify this equipment.
4. A high-speed printer located either in the warehouse or in the corporate headquarters for producing reports.
5. Video display terminals at each sales location, the number to be based on the volume of sales activity.

---

*The communications processor's function is to interact with the main central processing unit to minimize unnecessary communications overhead in the central processor.

VI. Technical Discussion

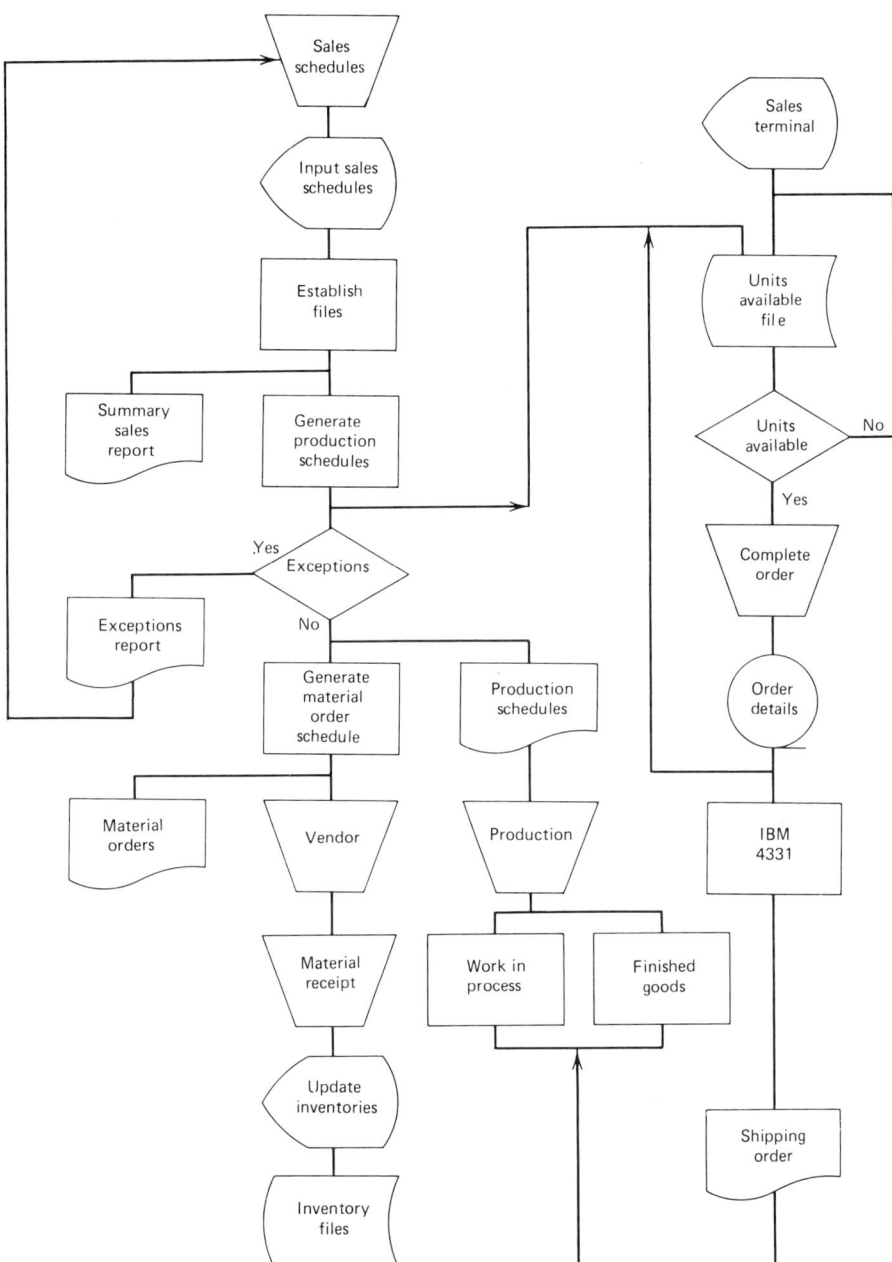

Figure 26. Logical processes flowchart of the proposed system.

6. Video display terminals in each factory for production interaction, as well as in the warehouse and the Purchasing Department to allow purchasing and inventory processing.
7. Video display terminals in the headquarter offices for management to control the system and get on-line, real-time information for decision making.

A diagram of the recommended equipment locations and physical data flow is presented in Figure 27.

VIII. IMPLEMENTATION

The tasks are to be performed in the order of their importance. A bar chart representing the time required for each implementation step is shown in Figure 28.

A. Organize Project Teams

Knowledgable user personnel from each affected area of the organization will be assigned to a team responsible for the development of specifications for the modules of the system that apply to their particular area. Data processing professionals also will be assigned to each team.

B. Prepare Detailed Specifications of the Needs of Each System

1. Inventory systems will be implemented first, because they are the greatest need in the Company. Since packaged inventory systems are available from many software vendors, I recommend that this software be purchased rather than developed in-house.
2. Because production scheduling must be known before details of units available can be produced for the sales locations, this application is to be developed next. This module is also needed for the material purchasing application. Since the components included in each unit are unique to SMC, I recommend that this system be developed in-house.
3. This is followed by the sales scheduling module. There are many good sales scheduling software packages on the market. Consequently, I recommend purchasing this application rather than developing it in-house.
4. Since the modules needed to support the remote sales location system—production scheduling and sales scheduling modules—must be complete at this juncture, it is important to ensure that the remote sales staff have enough information to sell as many of the Company's products as possible without overcommitting available production. Since the needs of this module are also unique to the Company, in-house software development is recommended.

VIII. Implementation

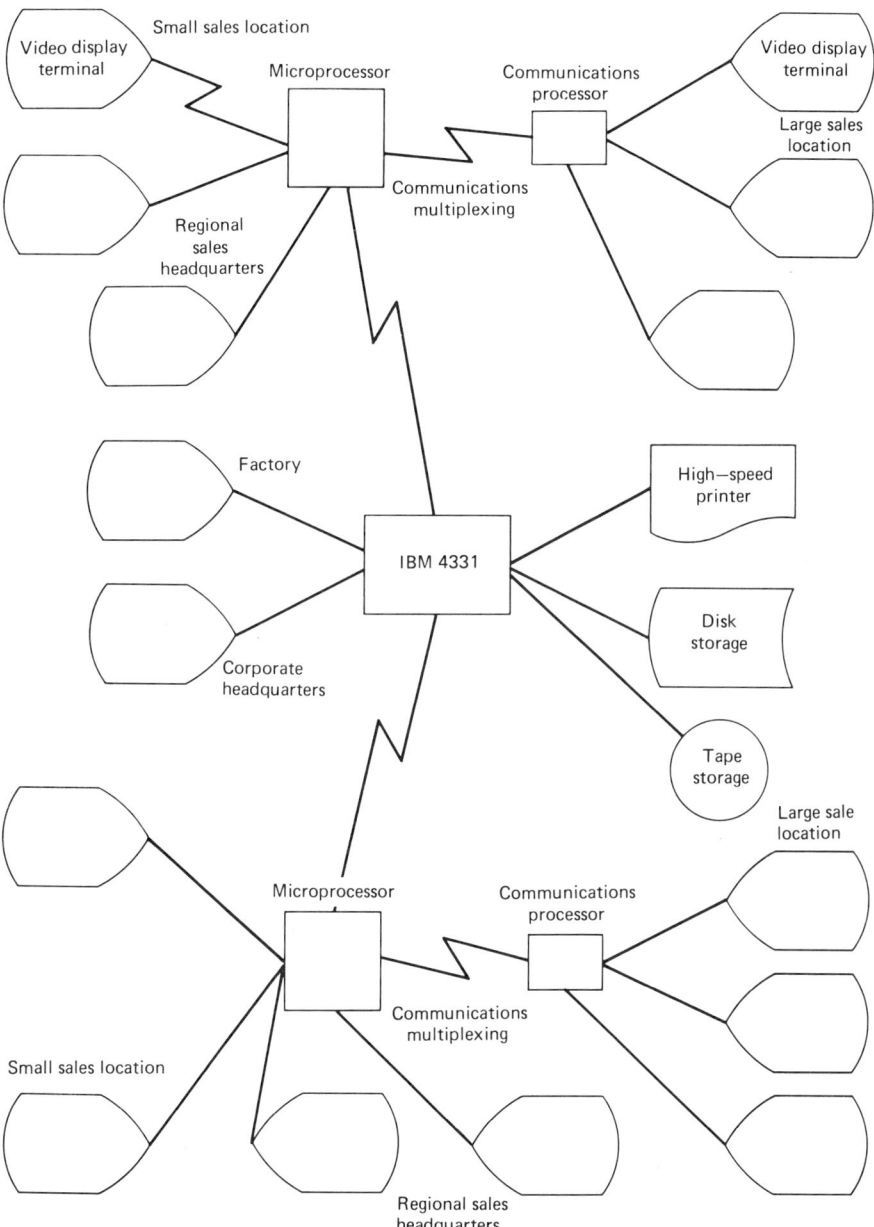

Figure 27. Hardware configurations and physical data flow of the proposed system.

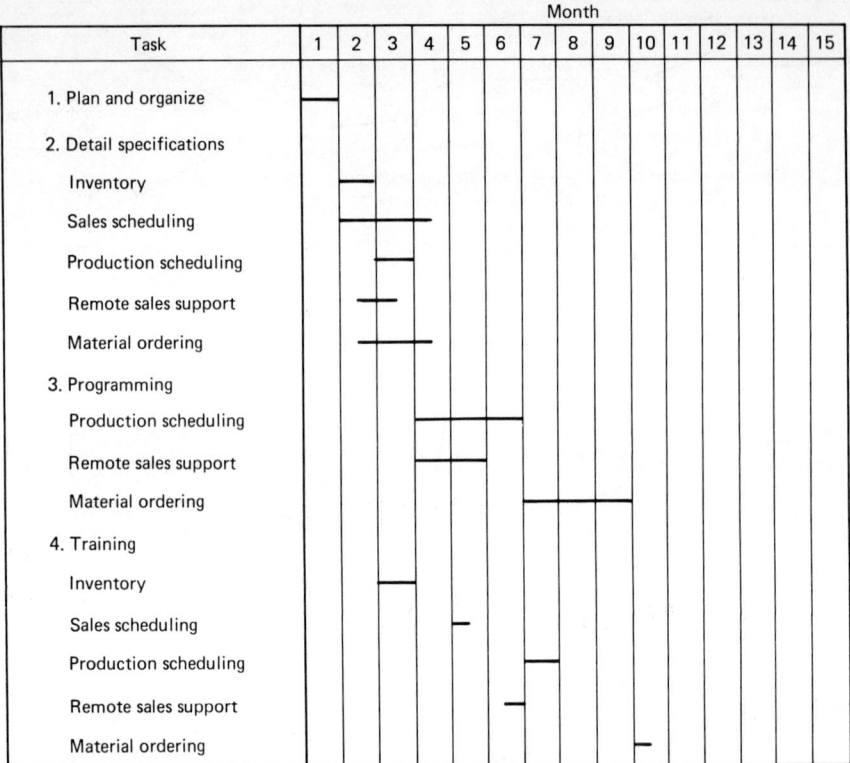

Figure 28. Implementation timetable of the proposed system.

5. Material ordering is the final module to be undertaken. The inventory system selected may include a module design to perform this function, but if it does not, a software vendor probably can be located that has a system versatile enough to meet this particular need of the Company.

IX. SECURITY AND CONTROL

The security and control of any computer system is a great concern to management. Consequently, the following areas need to be considered:

A. Physical Security

Physical security has been carefully studied by hardware manufacturers and independent computer personnel. The hardware being addressed in this study presents

IX. Security and Control

special security problems because of its distribution. The hardware to be installed in the warehouse would be located in a physically secure area, with only enough access to ensure safety in the event of fire. Accesses would be controlled by the use of magnetically coded key cards. Terminal accesses for terminals located outside this secure computer room would be controlled through (1) careful placement of each terminal in an area that is accessible only to authorized personnel, and (2) the use of keys to activate power within the terminal.

B. Data Security

Data security would be enhanced by using the following techniques:

1. Selective access to files based on file name, terminal address, and password authority. The access would be read-only in some cases, and read/write in others, depending on the user's designated authority.
2. All access to the system, successful and unsuccessful, would be logged on a tape for review by a system security person.
3. All files would be backed up daily, with copies of the files stored in off-site secure areas.
4. The system would generate a log-off for any VDT that had access to the system but had had no activity for a preestablished period of time, such as 10 minutes.

C. Logical Control

Logical control of system development would be maintained by performing all programming functions at the headquarters facility, releasing only the object code to the computer in the warehouse. If desired, it would be possible to remove the compiler from the system software in any machine other than the designated controlling unit.

D. Data Accuracy

Data accuracy would be enhanced in the following manner:

1. Each transaction would be edited for valid codes and ranges of values. Sales transactions, for example, would be edited for valid product code, customer code, the existence of a customer purchase order, and a valid price quoted by the salesperson.
2. Parity bit checks would be made on transmitted data to ensure accurate receipt of transmission.

3. To prevent manipulation of the sales file, a customer purchase order number would be required on each sales transaction, and the salesperson's access to the sales file would be on a read-only basis.
4. The person using the system would be held accountable for what he or she does. (It has been established that accountability is one of the greatest deterrents of computer theft and fraud.)

X. COST ANALYSIS

As requested by top management, the cost analysis section, including cost estimates for the proposed system as well as estimated qualitative benefits, has been given to the Company controller.

SAMPLE Hospital Management Information System
DESIGN SPECIFICATIONS

The following outputs are required from the computer system that is to be developed in response to the Riverview Hospital's Request For Proposal (RFP).

I. PRIORITY ONE REPORTS

1. The system shall be capable of providing *on-request reports* of a given patient's medical histories. Inputs (source documents) to the system for this information will be: the patient care records kept on each patient during his or her stay in the hospital; information obtained from other physicians and hospitals; and the patient's discharge record.
2. The system shall be capable of providing *on-request reports* highlighting critical factors of a given patient's medical history. Inputs to the system for this information will be: the patient care records, information from external medical sources, and the patient's discharge record. *Real-time response to these requests is essential.* Output locations must include the emergency room.
3. The system shall be capable of providing *reports of the location of each patient*. Inputs to the system for this will be from the admission records and the patient activity records. These are to be daily reports.
4. The system shall be capable of providing *daily summary reports that display the hospital occupancy status*. Included in these reports are the totals for the existing number of available beds, number of inpatients, number of scheduled patients for the next seven weeks (on a per week basis), and special requirements (e.g., single room with oxygen) mandating the relocation of large items of equipment. Inputs to the system for this information will be the admission records, discharge records, patient activity records, and reservation forms. Response to inquiries for these reports need not be in real-time.
5. The system shall be capable of providing *daily reports to the pharmacy,* listing all physicians' instructions for administration of medication for all patients in the hospital. The listing shall be sorted by hospital section and shall include

the patient's name and room number, the medication, the dosage, and the physician's name. Inputs for these data will be the doctors' orders on the patient activity records.

In addition to the listing, gummed labels will be produced for labeling each container of medication for each patient. *The reports and labels need to be provided on a real-time inquiry basis.*

6. The system shall be capable of providing *reports listing all administration of medication* to patients in a specified hospital section for a given time. The listings shall be sorted by room number. Inputs will be the physicians' orders on the patient care records. These reports will be generated in real-time, on demand. Output capability is required on every floor of the facility.

7. The system shall be capable of providing *reports listing all the laboratory tests* to be conducted within a specified time frame. Inputs will be the physicians' orders on the patient care records. Output capability shall exist in the analysis laboratory. The report will be generated in real-time.

8. The system shall be capable of generating *reports totaling the number of meals required* by each hospital section, by type of meal (breakfast, lunch, dinner). In addition, special diets shall be included in the reports. These reports shall contain all the information required by the hospital kitchen to prepare each meal served. Inputs to the system will be the patient care records, admission records, and discharge records. The reports shall be generated in real-time, on demand.

II. PRIORITY TWO REPORTS

1. The system shall be capable of generating *reports that meet the federal and state hospital accreditation requirements.* Inputs to the system will be the patients' admission and discharge records. These reports need not be in real-time.

2. The system shall be capable of generating *reports that meet the local Department of Public Health reporting requirements.* Inputs to the system will be the patient care records and the discharge records. These reports need to be produced on an overnight demand basis.

3. The system shall be capable of generating *patient bills*. Inputs to the system will be the analysis laboratory, the pharmacy, the patient care records, and unspecified documents used by the business office. The bills shall be produced on a scheduled monthly basis. In addition, records of all bills produced shall be kept indefinitely in microfiche form.

4. The system shall be capable of generating *insurance bills*. Inputs to the system will be the same sources as listed for patient bills. The bills shall be produced

III. Priority Three Reports

on a scheduled monthly basis. In addition, microfiche records of all bills produced shall be kept indefinitely.

5. The system shall be capable of producing *paychecks for the hospital staff*. Inputs will be time cards and manual entries by the business office. The paychecks will be printed twice a month, as scheduled.
6. The system shall have the capability to generate *General Ledger Statements*. The information shall be constructed from accounts receivable, accounts payable, and the patient care records, as well as other sources not yet defined.

III. PRIORITY THREE REPORTS

The system shall be capable of recording, storing, and listing the items that require reorder. That is, it shall have the capability to generate *Inventory Control Reports*. Inputs to the system will be the Inventory Control Forms. Input/output capabilities shall exist in the general stores area and the business office. These reports shall be generated on a scheduled weekly basis, except for the kitchen and the pharmacy. For the latter areas the same reports shall be generated daily.

PART THREE
Writing Other Types of Technical Material

Chapter Nine
Writing a Winning Technical Proposal

To ensure successful response to a Request For Proposal (RFP) or a Request For Quotation (RFQ),* many enterprises that respond regularly to RFPs within their area of specialization have a "proposal committee." This committee makes bid/no-bid as well as policy decisions, and has direct responsibility for preparing solicited† proposals.

The membership of a structured proposal committee may consist of a marketing director, proposal manager, proposal coordinator, technical editor, tasking and scheduling section leader, pricing section leader, and management section leader. Or it may consist of only a marketing director, proposal manager, and coordinator. The size of a proposal committee or team, however, does not necessarily mean that an effective proposal will be produced. It is the combination of qualifications and dedication of the technical proposal team that counts.

But whether the team is structured or not, whether the team consists of 3 or 12 members, the goal is the same: produce a winning proposal. And if the proposal is well-written, meaningful and concise, has a spacious format with functional illustrations, is logically organized and easily referenced, *and* cost-attractive, it is likely to be a winner.

---

*An RFP or an RFQ in the DP field is a document that describes in detail the software system and/or DP service and/or hardware a government agency or a private corporation wants to obtain. The purpose of an RFP or RFQ is to elicit proposals from qualified vendors or service companies who can respond satisfactorily to specific requirements within the economic and other constraints stated in the RFP.

†Solicited proposals are bids that respond to an RFP/RFQ, while unsolicited proposals are bids that approach a corporation or agency on the vendor's or service company's own initiative. Since writing a proposal is a costly project, both as to time and money, unsolicited proposals, besides being quite similar to solicited proposals, are almost nonexistent. Therefore, this chapter deals only with writing solicited proposals.

NOTE: If the proposal concerns hard products, such as a large mainframe, mini or micro computers, or peripheral equipment, the content of the proposal varies somewhat. The sections "Background/Statement of the Problem" and "Objectives and Statement of Work," for example—both of which will be detailed later—would only have the headings "Background" and "Objectives" respectively, and would discuss the background and objectives of specific hardware.

Depending on the size and complexity of the proposed system (if the RFP is for the procurement of a system), a proposal usually consists of one, two, or three parts. Exceptions are proposals to government agencies, which may be comprised of 10 to 12 parts contained in four to five manuals.

Regardless of how many or how few parts the technical proposal consists of, the front section is always made up of the following items, in the following sequence.

1. Transmittal/cover letter.
2. Title page.
3. Table of contents.
4. List of illustrations.

The illustrations may include organization charts, tables, flowcharts, task and time schedules, and sample reports, as well as relevant forms to be used.

Because proposals' size and format depend upon the RFPs they respond to, and because RFPs vary so much from industry to industry and from agency to agency, two representative proposals will be discussed: one smaller and simpler, and one larger and more complex.

Examples of sample applications follow the discussions.

1. THE SMALL AND SIMPLE PROPOSAL

Within this category there are two types of proposal: formal and informal.

The Small and Simple Proposal

a. **The formal small proposal.** Because it is proposing a relatively simple task in response to a verbal or written RFP, the formal small proposal is usually contained in one manual, consisting of 6 to 60 pages.

Following is a detailed description of what should be included in this type of proposal.

1. Transmittal or cover letter.
2. Title page.
3. Table of contents.
4. List of illustrations.
5. Background/statement of the problem.
6. Objectives and statement of work.
7. Technical approach.
8. Project management and staffing plan.
9. Qualifications.
10. Pricing schedule.

THE TRANSMITTAL LETTER IS A CRUCIAL PART OF THE PROPOSAL

1. **Transmittal/cover letter.** This item is mandatory, regardless of the length of the proposal. In small proposals, where there's no need for an introduction section, the transmittal letter becomes one of the most important parts of the proposal. It sets the tone of the whole document in addition to providing the initial impression of your company to the customer's nontechnical proposal reviewer. Consequently, the transmittal letter must be short (no longer than a page and a half), and it must state concisely the subject of the proposal as well as the reason for submitting the document.

Usual components of the transmittal letter (on your company's letterhead) are:

ELEMENTS OF THE TRANSMITTAL LETTER

- Name of the firm or agency the proposal is submitted to.
- Title of the proposal, its identifying case number, and the closing date for the RFP.
- One or two short sentences, stating why your company is particularly qualified to bid for the project.

- A terse statement indicating that you understand the objectives of the project, and that your company would welcome an opportunity to discuss any part of the proposal.
- A listing of the major sections in the proposal, what they are comprised of, and if there are any supplements, include them in the list.
- Name, title, and signature of the person (usually the president of the company) who is authorized to legally bind your company to the requirements and obligations contained in the proposal.
- Name(s) of the liaison person(s) whom the firm or agency may contact during the proposal evaluation period.
- A statement that the pricing schedule section is being submitted separately, if the RFP so specifies it.

2. **Title page.** Has been discussed previously.
3. **Table of contents.** Has been discussed previously.
4. **List of illustrations.** Has been discussed previously.
5. **Background/statement of the problem.** This section presents in precise, vivid language the background or the problem(s) that the proposal is addressing. This is followed by describing the key requirements of the company or agency based on specifications in the RFP, as interpreted by the bidder.

PROBLEM AND WORK STATEMENT

6. **Objectives/statement of work.** This section states the overall purpose of the proposed project, and provides a compact description of how you intend to accomplish the specific objectives.

PROFILE OF THE PROPOSED SYSTEM

7. **Technical approach.** This section provides a detailed technical description of the proposed system to meet the potential customer's exact requirements.

8. **Project management and staffing plan.** This section presents the project organization, including the latest or-

The Small and Simple Proposal

YOUR PLAN TO MANAGE THE PROJECT EFFICIENTLY AND ON TIME

ganization chart of your company and (if applicable) of the department proposing the system. Include the resumés of personnel who will serve on the proposed project, and their areas of responsibility and expertise. In addition, provide a plan for organizing the selected staff's activities. The organization plan shows the customer that your company can manage a timely and efficient completion of all the assignments stated in the Statement of Work and the Technical Approach sections.

9. Qualifications. This section displays your company's background, and lists projects relevant to the proposed system that your company has been and is working on.

YOUR PRICE QUOTATION FOR THE PROJECT

10. Pricing schedule. This section provides detailed cost schedule/price quotation of each task, as well as the cost of any optional feature, *plus* the cost benefits of the proposed system.

b. **The informal small proposal.** This free-style proposal describes the automated (or even manual) system by which you propose to resolve the customer's problems or need. In such a proposal, even the transmittal letter may be quite informal. In fact, this type of proposal need not conform to any format as long as it is concise and clear.

The sample formal small proposal that follows is for submission to a supplier of parts for the plumbing industry.

SAMPLE Small Formal Proposal

COMMERCIAL DP SERVICES, INC.
44 MONTGOMERY STREET
SAN FRANCISCO, CA 94104

October 7, 1981

Mr. Arnold Barron
President
A-A Company, Inc.
North Michigan Avenue
Chicago, IL 60611

        RE: REQUEST FOR PROPOSAL NO: 80-018
        CLOSING DATE: OCTOBER 8, 1981

Dear Mr. Barron:

Commercial DP Services, Inc. (CDSI) is pleased to submit this proposal for "A Total Business System" in response to your above RFP. CDSI is eminently qualified to undertake this effort by our experience, resources, and expertise in the commercial minicomputer field.

In addition to meeting your requirements, we offer various cost-effective options for your consideration.

Section I of the attached proposal presents a statement of the problem that is being addressed in the proposed project. Section II outlines the objectives and states how we intend to accomplish them. Section III describes the technical approach for meeting your requirements. Section IV discusses the project organization and staffing, including brief biographies of the staff proposed for this assignment. Section V details CDSI's qualifications, including brief summaries of a number of relevant projects performed by the CDSI staff.

No cost or pricing data are included in the technical proposal. This information, in accordance with the RFP, is submitted under separate cover.

The management of CDSI would welcome the opportunity to answer any questions in regard to the proposed system.

As President of CDSI, I have the authority to legally bind the company to the requirements and obligations contained in our proposal.

Sincerely,

Robert Western
President

RW/sf

PROPOSAL TO THE MANAGEMENT OF A-A COMPANY, INC., FOR A TOTAL BUSINESS SYSTEM

October 7, 1981

COMMERCIAL DP SERVICES, INC.
44 MONTGOMERY STREET
SAN FRANCISCO, CA 94104

CONTENTS

Section		Page
I	Statement of the Problem	156
II	Objectives and Statement of Work	156
III	Technical Approach	157
IV	Project Management and Staffing Plan	158

ILLUSTRATIONS

Figure		
29	Proposed Business System Task Structure	157
30	Task and Time Schedule Chart	158
31	Project Organization Chart	159

I. STATEMENT OF THE PROBLEM

According to the RFP, the rapid growth of A-A Company necessitates the automation of the firm's manual method of processing order entries, controlling inventory, and attending to job follow-ups. Increased sales volume makes the manual processing of such tasks as card file job follow-up, for example, quite difficult and time-consuming. Moreover, the company is losing some customers because of delays in filling orders. (Much too often the orders cannot be found because the job cards have been misfiled or lost.) Furthermore, management needs timely and accurate management and administrative reports for decision making. And finally, the company wants to process the accounts payable, accounts receivable, payroll, and tax reports in-house, instead of using an outside computer service company, as they have been for the past three years.

Based upon the above, the A-A Company's key requirements are: an in-house medium or minicomputer system that will: (1) boost productivity, (2) provide economy of operation, (3) handle all applications of the company, (4) furnish an English-like user language, so that management and non-DP personnel can use the system in addition to the programming staff, and (5) produce various management reports. Moreover, the system has to be flexible and have the capability to be upgraded easily. This last feature is needed for the anticipated increase in the volume of sales in the not too distant future.

II. OBJECTIVES AND STATEMENT OF WORK

The objectives of this project are: selecting, analyzing, evaluating, and implementing an efficient medium or a minicomputer system for the A-A Company that will resolve current problems and have the capability to meet future expansions.

To accomplish these objectives, CDSI will:

1. Analyze and document A-A's present system.
2. Study in-depth various medium-size computer systems, such as HP3000, as well as minicomputer systems such as IBM 4331, for compatibility with A-A's needs. Evaluate the performance, economy, and other key features of the systems under consideration.
3. Provide A-A's management oral and written presentations on the results of the study and the feasibility of the recommended system.
4. Implement the selected system and develop various applications to meet the company's requirements. The computer system will include order entry, inventory control, job follow-ups, job cost estimates, production scheduling,

III. Technical Approach

sales analysis and forecast, cost accounting, and payroll applications or subsystems. It will also generate timely and accurate management reports on-request basis.

5. Provide a user's guide and on-site training for the programming staff who will operate the system as well as for the nonprogramming staff who will use the system via an English-like, nonprocedural language.

III. TECHNICAL APPROACH

CDSI's proposed methodology for undertaking this project for A-A Company is described below. Based on many years of experience, CDSI is proposing to accomplish the project in six tasks and within a 6 month time-frame. The first figure presents the System Task Structure, and the second figure displays the Task and Time Schedule for the project (see Figures 29 and 30).

A description of the six tasks follows:

Task 1: Analysis of A-A Company's Current System. To develop a satisfactory computer system, CDSI must understand the company's flow of work, the current manual processing, and the problems unique to the plumbing parts suppliers industry. Consequently, we will study, analyze and document the company's current system.

Task 2: Evaluation and Analysis of Appropriate Computer Systems. CDSI will evaluate and analyze selected medium and minicomputers as to costs, performance, service, and compatibility. This method will enable us to match your needs to the best hardware and software available within a reasonable price range.

Task 3: Presentation of Findings. CDSI will provide A-A Company management with oral and written presentations of our assessment of various systems.

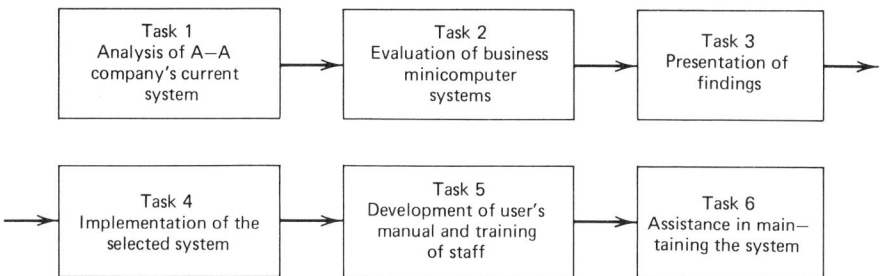

Figure 29. System task structure.

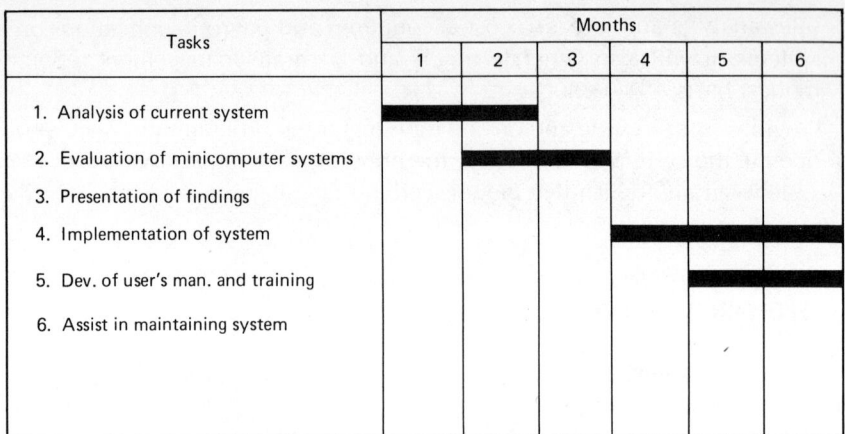

Figure 30. Task and time schedule chart.

We will describe in simple, direct language the hardware, software, personnel requirements, and maintenance costs, as well as the cost-benefits of the systems under consideration.

Task 4: Implementation of the Selected System. Once A-A management decides which one of the recommended systems to buy or lease, we shall modify the available software and our business applications programs to run on the selected hardware, and finally, implement the system.

Task 5: Development of User's Guide and Training of Staff. CDSI will provide a user's guide that will contain all the steps necessary for successful usage of the computer system. Moreover, the document will be an easy-to-read, easy-to-reference guide for both management as well as the non-DP personnel. In addition, CDSI will provide comprehensive training to the newly hired programming staff to ensure that the system will be operated efficiently and economically.

Task 6: Assistance in Maintaining the System. For 6 months after the successful implementation of the selected system, CDSI will provide assistance on a "when-needed" basis in the maintenance of the system.

IV. PROJECT MANAGEMENT AND STAFFING PLAN

Under the CDSI project management system each project leader reports and is accountable for all deliverables to the Project Director, Robert Wilson. Mr. Wilson, who reports to the President of CDSI, reviews and monitors the status of each

IV. Project Management and Staffing Plan

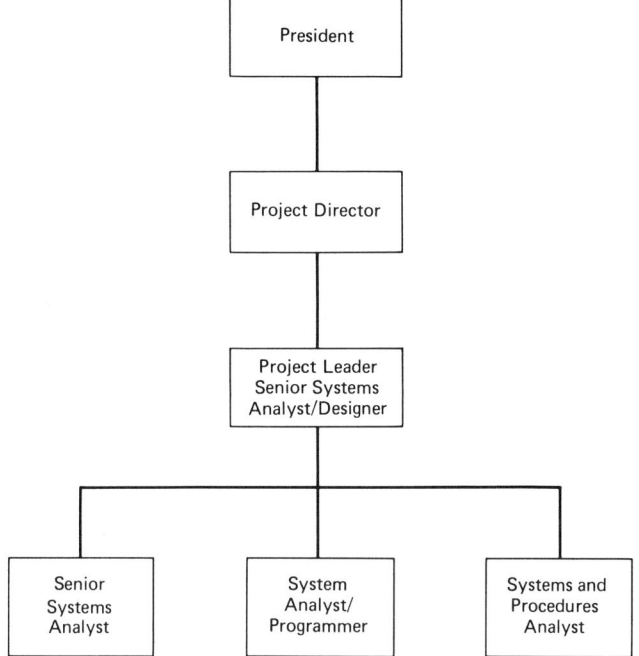

Figure 31. Project organization.

project. CDSI's staffing plan is designed to utilize our resources to the fullest, according to specific areas of technical expertise.

The proposed project would be led by Thomas Day, Sr. Systems Analyst/Designer, assisted by Rod McKay, Sr. Systems Analyst, Laurence Warner, Programmer/Analyst, and Bruce Barker, Systems and Procedures Analyst. Biographical sketches of these key personnel—all from the Systems Development Department—are presented on the following pages.* In addition, a simplified project organization chart is shown in the third figure (Figure 31).

---

*To avoid boring the reader with insignificant material, the biographical sketches and the bidding company's qualifications have been left out of this proposal.

2. THE LARGE AND COMPLEX PROPOSAL

The sheer volume (100 to 1500 pages) of a large and complex proposal makes it both a demanding and time-consuming project. And although responses to government and commercial RFPs require somewhat different formats, in general, the sections, headings, subheadings, the quality of writing, and most importantly the substance in most winning proposals are similar if not the same.

Following is a detailed description of what this type of proposal usually consists of.

1. Transmittal letter.
2. Title page.
3. Table of contents.
4. List of illustrations.
5. Introduction.
6. Executive summary.
7. Corporate background/business organization.
8. Technical approach.
9. Project management and staffing plan.
10. Pricing schedule.

a. Transmittal letter. This section is quite similar in both large and small proposals. (See Section 1.1 in this chapter.)

b. Title page. See earlier discussion.

c. Table of contents. See earlier discussion.

d. List of illustrations. See earlier discussion.

IMPRESS THE CONTRACT ADMINISTRATOR WITH YOUR INTRODUCTION

e. Introduction. Equal to or perhaps more important than the transmittal letter is the introduction. This section gives a capsule description of your company and tells how you intend to respond to the RFP, as well as why

The Large and Complex Proposal 161

you are uniquely qualified to perform the proposed project. It indicates that you completely understand the requirements stated in the RFP, and that you are looking forward to the opportunity of meeting the potential customer/client's systems needs.

NOTE: This is where the company submitting the proposal may lose to its competitor, unless the person writing the proposal has defined and is aiming the material at the individual who first reads the introduction: the Contract Administrator. (See Part One, Chapter 3.)

MAKE EVERY WORD COUNT IN YOUR EXECUTIVE SUMMARY

f. **Executive summary.** This section presents the client management with an overview of your entire proposal. It describes—without going into technical details—your management's methods of meeting the requirements of the RFP's system within the stated financial and time constraints. Examples of features that may be included are: method of design, development, modification, implementation, operations/maintenance (only if the RFP calls for such tasks), method of approach, processing location, method of processing, timing of major milestones, and summary benefits for the client.

g. **Corporate background/business organization.** In this section you provide the client (especially if it's a government agency) financial and other information about your company, including a detailed statement about your company's experience that qualifies you to undertake and complete the proposed project.

Each experience is described in terms of work performed, including the scope and complexity of the project; the yearly transaction volume; the time period in which the services were performed; the size of the manual and computer operations; and the person-months of effort expended in the design, development, and implementation phases.

In addition, you list the names, addresses, and telephone numbers of organizations who may be contacted for your referenced business experience. Finally, you state your company's location and the size of your data processing facilities and display the structure of your company/corporation through an organization chart.

THE GIST OF YOUR PROPOSAL IS THE TECHNICAL APPROACH SECTION

h. **Technical approach.** This section is the "meat" of the technical proposal. Here you detail the system that you propose to design and develop, or the client's existing operation system that you intend to use. You display flowcharts of the proposed system and, if you are going to use the client's existing system, you explain the extent of design and development required to convert the system to the particular need of the client. You also list assumptions or constraints that you believe will possibly affect the project.

You present a breakdown of all work (including manual processing) into major subtasks; estimates of your company's efforts by staffs' skill and level; and the elapsed time involved in the completion of subtasks.

You provide a network diagram such as Critical Path Method (CPM) or Project Evaluation Review Technique (PERT), or equivalent, indicating all major subtasks and milestone dates critical to the completion of the project on schedule. (See page 170 for sample CPM.)

You describe the hardware configuration to support the proposed system (not forgetting a plan for backup), and your method of documenting the system. Finally, you indicate how you intend to implement and operate the proposed system. (See page 132 for sample hardware configuration chart.)

i. **Project management and staffing plan.** See Section 1.8 of this chapter for a description of this item.

ACCURATE COSTS SECTION IS A CRUCIAL PART OF YOUR PROPOSAL

j. **Pricing schedule.** This section details the exact cost of each task in the proposed system. It consists of price quotation on the system development and facility development, if appropriate, operations charges, if appropriate, and the cost of optional features, *plus* cost benefits of the proposed system for the potential client.

The Large and Complex Proposal

The pricing schedule is almost always instructed (in the RFP) to be submitted in a separate manual because the cost data of a large proposal invariably goes directly to the controller or financial administrator.

Because of the prevalence of Management Information System (MIS) type of computer systems processing applications in commercial, government, and education fields, and because the National Health Care Program looms large on the horizon, the following drastically abbreviated sample application of a large and complex proposal is for a state Medicaid Management Information System (MMIS). The format, however, is the same for other government or commercial file management or data base system, as well as for distributed data processing network.

SAMPLE Large, Complex Proposal
COMMERCIAL DP SERVICES, INC.
44 MONTGOMERY STREET
SAN FRANCISCO, CA 94104

March 18, 1982

Mr. H. H. Smith, Director
Division of Procurement
Department of Health and Human Resources
Street _____
City _____
State and zip code _____

                              Reference: RFP Number 21–04–37R

                              Closing Date: March 19, 1982

Dear Mr. Smith:

Commercial DP Services, Inc. (CDSI) herein submits this proposal to the State of _____ in response to the above referenced solicitation. This proposal is for the design, development, implementation, and operation of a Medicaid Management Information System (MMIS) for the State's Title XIX Medical Assistance Program. As requested, CDSI's response is in three volumes. Seven copies of Volume I and II and two copies of Volume III are attached for your evaluation and kind consideration.

Volume I, the "Technical Proposal," describes the management overview of the project, as well as a technically sound and cost-effective approach to satisfy the State's requirements.

Volume II, the "Appendices," presents the technical details of the proposed system, and provides examples of the reports that the system will generate.

Volume III, the "Cost Schedule," provides the State with CDSI's price quotations.

We believe that we are notably qualified by experience, resources, and management processes to satisfy the State's requirements, and provide a successful, cost-beneficial system for the State.

We fully understand the State's requirements, and appreciate the opportunity to bid for a project of this magnitude. Moreover, we will be pleased to answer questions about any item in the proposal.

The undersigned is authorized to legally bind the company to the requirements and obligations contained in this proposal.

Very truly yours,

Robert Western
President

RW/sj

PROPOSAL TO THE STATE OF _____

DIVISION OF PROCUREMENT

DEPARTMENT OF HEALTH AND HUMAN RESOURCES

DESIGN, DEVELOPMENT, IMPLEMENTATION, AND OPERATION OF THE STATE TITLE XIX MEDICAID MANAGEMENT INFORMATION SYSTEM (MMIS)

RFP No. 21-04-37R
March 18, 1982

COMMERCIAL DP SERVICES, INC.
44 MONTGOMERY STREET
SAN FRANCISCO, CA 94104

CONTENTS

Section	Page

I. Introduction 168
II. Executive Summary 168
III. Business Organization/Background 169
IV. Technical Approach 172
V. Project Management and Staffing Plan 174

ILLUSTRATIONS

Figure

34 CDSI Chart 174
35 Critical Path Method Chart 176
36 Facility Preparation. Task and Time Schedule 177
37 DP Requirements Definition. Task and Time Schedule 177
38 Manual Processing Implementation. Task and Time Schedule 177

I. INTRODUCTION

In response to the State's Request For Proposal (RFP) No. 21–04–37R, CDSI is pleased to present a detailed discussion of its qualifications to act as fiscal intermediary for the State's Medicaid program. We are also providing details of our currently operating Medicaid Management Information System (MMIS), which we will customize to the State's requirements. This in-depth presentation of CDSI's products, as well as our experience, organizational management and administrative ability, will show our progressive approach to achieve the objectives of the State in the most cost-efficient manner.

A comprehensive discussion of the benefits of the proposed system—as it applies to the State, its providers, and eligible recipients—is presented in subsequent sections of this proposal.

CDSI, having established a reputation for the design, development, implementation, and operation of successful MMISs on schedule and within budget, assures the State that this proposal is completely responsive to the State's RFP. Moreover, CDSI is totally committed to provide the highest quality system to administer the State's program.

II. EXECUTIVE SUMMARY

A. Purpose.

This section describes the management methods to be used to meet the requirements of the design, development, implementation, and operational phases of the upcoming contract for the State's Title XIX Medical Assistance Program (Medicaid).

In our management methods we emphasize three factors: highly qualified, experienced personnel, responsiveness, and accountability. The value of this approach has been repeatedly demonstrated in the capability of CDSI program administration and claims processing to serve government, commercial, and industrial accounts.

CDSI can provide the following management and technical capabilities:

- Experience in administering large-scale Medicaid programs.
- On-site facilities and staffs.
- Experience in specialized data processing systems to monitor and control the provision of medical services in a Medical Assistance Program.
- Adherence to data management standards, practices, and reporting requirements stated in the RFP.

III. Business Organization/Background

- Extensive experience in the establishment and implementation of Peer Review (a selected group of distinguished physicians and pharmacists within the State who are asked to review cases that appear on the exception reports), and in the analysis of overutilization, fraud, and abuse of the State's Medicaid Program.

B. Summary of Benefits

- Accuracy of claims processing.
- Cost-effectiveness.
- Correct and rapid payments to the providers.
- Strict control over security, confidentiality, and integrity of data.
- Informational data for the providers on their remittance.
- Comprehensive, easy-to-read monthly reports to the State on every vital phase of the Medicaid Program.
- Maximum flexibility to meet immediate needs of the State in regard to the Medicaid Program through AD HOC reports, upon request.

III. BUSINESS ORGANIZATION/BACKGROUND

A. Purpose

This section provides the required information about CDSI and the status of the organization.

B. Organization Policies

CDSI is an experienced and successful company that has established an excellent reputation for delivering on schedule and within budget MMIS and other health care systems to several eastern and midwestern states. Thus CDSI brings to the State's Medical Assistance Program a diversified background of problem solving and data processing capabilities resulting from the design, development, implementation, and operation of similar systems.

A wide range of consulting projects in the health care field has provided CDSI with an in-depth knowledge of activities, ranging from utilization review systems and procedures to management of health maintenance organizations.

CDSI is a California company with headquarters and data processing facilities in San Francisco. (The organization chart of our company follows.) (See Figure 32.)

In addition, a summary of current major state and commercial contracts, together with their respective claims processing volumes and contact references, follows.

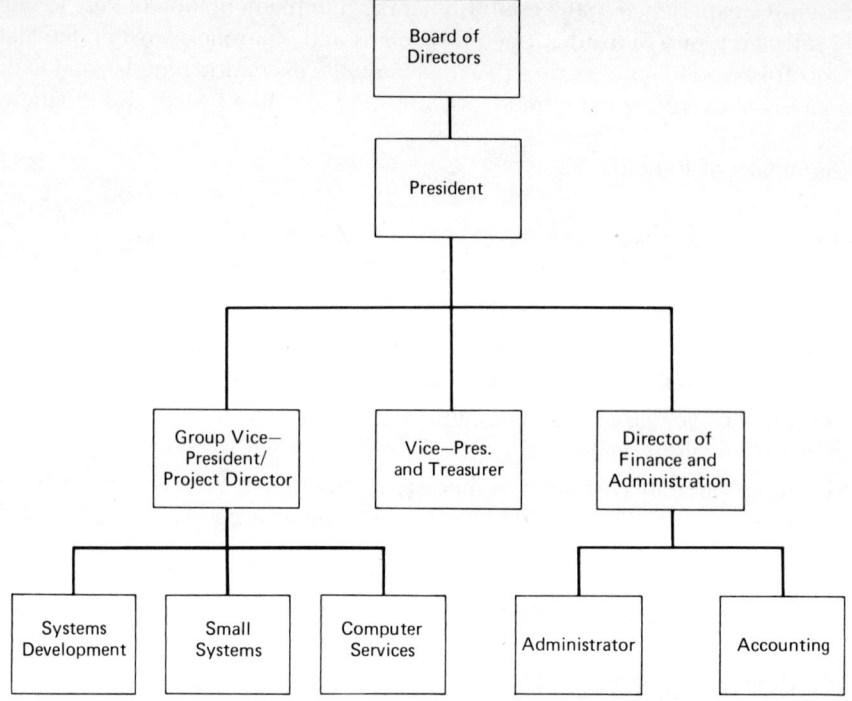

Figure 32. Commercial DP Services, Inc. organization chart.

III. Business Organization/Background

SUMMARY OF CONTRACTS

Client	Contacts	Monthly Claim Volume	Type of Claim	Contract Period
State ____ Medicaid Program	Name: Address: Telephone:	550,000	All provider types	10/78 ongoing
State ____ Medicaid Program	Name: Address: Telephone:	200,000	All provider types	12/74 to 7/77
State ____ Medicaid Program	Name: Address: Telephone:	308,000	All provider types	7/75 ongoing
Company ____	Name: Address: Telephone:	40,000	Prescription drugs	6/69 to 5/75
Company ____	Name: Address: Telephone:	35,000	All provider types	3/80 ongoing
State ____ Public Employee Health and Welfare Fund (Self-Insured)	Name: Address Telephone:	50,000	Dental	11/79 ongoing

IV. TECHNICAL APPROACH

A. Purpose

This section describes the proposed system including the manual and automated data processing functions starting with the receipt of the claim forms from the providers, until payment or other disposition is made. Editing, validating, pricing, as well as utilization review and management reporting, are discussed at length. File descriptions and report contents are detailed under each subsystem.

B. System Description

The effectiveness of a system must be evaluated not only by its capability to meet current user needs, but also by its flexibility and capability for rapid expansion without costly reprogramming.

Keeping this in mind, the herein offered MMIS was designed by CDSI staff to provide management an innovative and quality control health care delivery program with a businesslike approach to the problem of cost control. An overview diagram of the proposed MMIS follows (Figure 33).

The proposed system is discussed in seven subsections. They are:

1. Manual processing and data entry.
2. Recipient subsystem.
3. Provider subsystem.
4. Claims processing subsystem.
5. Reference file subsystem.
6. Surveillance and utilization review subsystem.
7. Management and administrative reporting subsystem.

NOTE: For the sake of economy of text, only a terse description of each subsection is given below.

1. Manual Processing and Data Entry

    a. Manual processing—involves screening claims received from providers; establishing batch controls; assigning control numbers to each claim; microfilming the claims; and forwarding the claims to data entry.

    b. Data entry—Keys in and verifies claims, and maintains batch integrity via assigned batch control numbers.

IV. Technical Approach

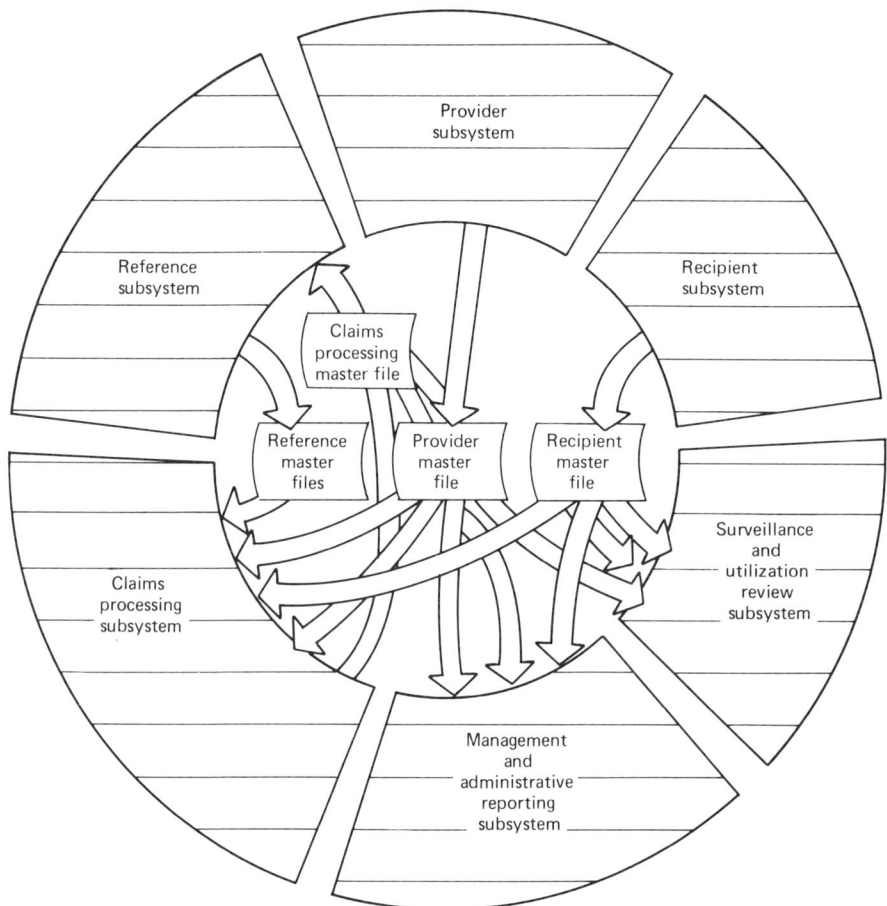

Figure 33. Medicaid management information system overview diagram.

2. **Recipient Subsystem.** The main purpose of the Recipient Subsystem is to maintain a current computer file of eligible recipients for eligibility verification in the Claims Processing Subsystem.
3. **Provider Subsystem.** The main purpose of the Provider Subsystem is to edit, update, delete, change, and validate claims from providers in order to update provider master file before the next claims processing cycle.
4. **Claims Processing Subsystem.** This subsystem uses the files maintained in the Recipient, Provider, and Reference File subsystems, and its main purpose is to process and pay valid claims for providers.

5. **Reference File Subsystem.** The main purpose of this subsystem is to maintain computerized medical code and price list with changes, additions, or deletions.
6. **Surveillance and Utilization Review Subsystem (SURS).** The main purpose of this subsystem is to provide the means for computerized detection of patterns of medical practices that vary from the norm.
7. **Management and Administrative Reporting Subsystem (MARS).** The main purpose of this subsystem is to provide the contractor and the State Health Care Department management with timely statistical reports about the program fiscal status and the operation of the system.

V. PROJECT MANAGEMENT AND STAFFING PLAN

Our project organization is task oriented, and the management team was selected from among CDSI specialists with extensive experience in the particular tasks to which they have been assigned.

This section presents the key members of the management team who will assist the project director in the proposed project. In addition to these specialists, the entire CDSI management and professional and technical staff will be available to the MMIS personnel for consultation.

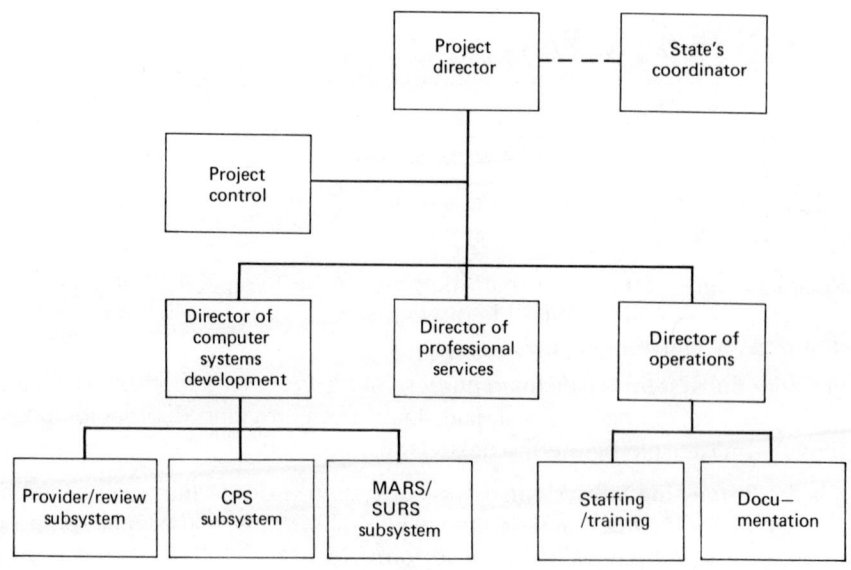

Figure 34. Project organization.

V. Project Management and Staffing Plan

Instead of a lengthy description of our project management and staffing plan, we are visually presenting how we envision the project organization and the level of staff who would be communicating with the State's Coordinator (Figure 34). Next, in Figure 35, we provide via a Critical Path Method (CPM) chart a clear and concise picture of the sequence of each task. This is followed by task and time schedule tables that show how much time various tasks will take. Figure 36 displays how many tasks and how long facility preparation will take. Figure 37 is a breakdown on the tasks and the time these tasks will take in defining EDP requirements of the State Medicaid. Figure 38 shows the tasks and the time these tasks will take in implementing manual processing for the MMIS. And finally, we are providing a summary of our key personnel in an easy-to-read table form.

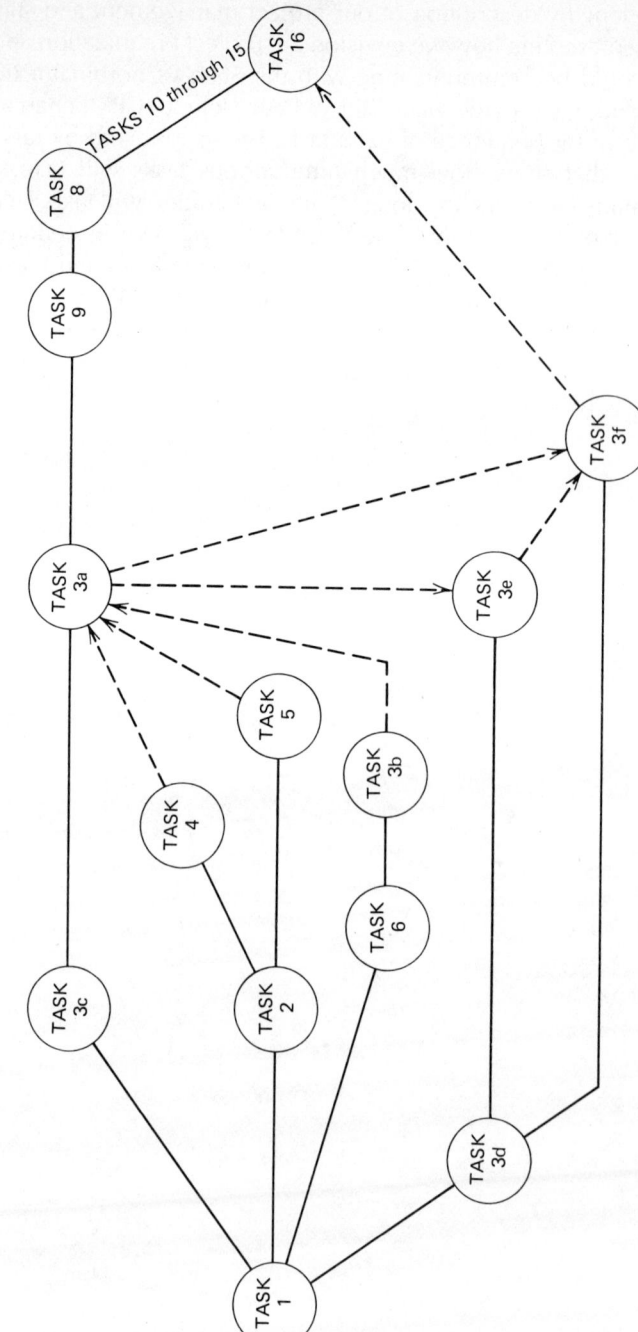

Figure 35. Critical path method chart.

V. Project Management and Staffing Plan 177

Number	Subtask Description	Person–days C	Person–days M	Weeks from Contract Award 1–14
1	Facility acquisition		55	Acquisition / Facility modifications
2	Acquire forms and supplies		55	
3	Hiring supervisory and clerical staff	5	10	
4	Project director's managerial activities		65	
5	Progress reports to the state (Bi–Weekly)		50	Ongoing
	Total person days	5	235	

Figure 36. Task and time schedule. Facility preparation.

Number	Subtask Description	Systems Analyst Person–days	Weeks from Contract Award 1–14
1.1	Analyze state medicaid regulations	5	
1.2	Define system requirements based on regulations	7	
1.3	Analyze current state processing requirements	7	
1.4	Define system requirements	7	
1.5	Document system design requirements	2	
1.6	Finalize work plan and state approval	2	
	Total person days	30	

Figure 37. Task and time schedule. EDP requirements definition.

Number	Subtask Description	Person–days C	Person–days M	Weeks from Contract Award 1–14
1	Modify manual claims processing system		10	
2	Prepare internal operations manual		35	
3	Modify accounting and office systems procedures		20	
4	Prepare accounting and office manual		20	
5	Train managers and supervisors		25	
6	Train clerical personnel	5	5	
	Total person days	5	115	

Figure 38. Task and time schedule. Manual processing implementation.

SUMMARY OF KEY PERSONNEL

Name	Assignment	Education	Summary of Directly Applicable Experience
Doyle, Brian	Project Director	B.A. English, Mathematics	Project Director. Previously in charge of development and implementation of the ongoing MMIS in the State of _____.
Woods, Don	Program Manager	B.S. Business Administration	MMIS Program Manager. Previous responsibility as Assistant to MMIS Program Manager.
Forsyth, Alan	Director of Operations	B.A. Business Administration M.B.A.	MMIS Director of Operations. Previously MMIS Operations Manager and Contract Liaison Officer.
Rakin, Edward	Project Control Administrator	B.S. Business Administration/ Accounting	MMIS Project Control Administrator. Formerly Controller for Commercial Program Data Center.
Jones, Ray	Director of Computer Systems Development	B.A. Business Administration	Director of Computer Systems Development. Formerly Technical Services Manager and administrator of a major computerized medical claims processing development project.

Stone, Ralph	Health Services Consultant	B.S., Pharmacy; M.P.H., Health Administration and Planning	MMIS Professional Services Consultant and consulting pharmacist.
Anderson, Daniel	Systems Support	B.S. Physics	Senior Systems Analyst with responsibility in implementation of SURS and MARS.
Wolfe, Wm., M.D.	Director of Professional Services	M.D.	Director of Professional Services. Chief Medical Consultant; provides consultation on Professional Standard Review, Patterns of Treatment, Provider Relations, and Patient Confidentiality.
Haas, Kenneth, M.D.	Consulting Psychiatrist	M.D.	Medical Committee Health Care Program. Utilization and quality control studies.
Miller, John	Technical Liaison for Medicaid Program	B.S. Mathematics	Technical Liaison for Medicaid Program. Formerly Systems Engineer and Technical Manager in another MMIS project.

179

Chapter Ten
Writing Policy and Standards Manuals

Company manuals should be developed and executed with the following goals in mind: functionality, readability, and flexibility. The accomplishment of these aims is essential to communicate clearly to personnel what the management formulated policies, standards, and procedures are.

Company manuals fall into three main categories: (1) policy manuals, (2) standards manuals, and (3) procedures manuals. Within these three categories there may be several subcategories. In a large enterprise the set of policy manuals, for example, may consist of the following volumes: Personnel Policy (hiring, promoting, transferring, terminating, etc.), Sales Policy, Merchandising Policy, Security and Control Policy, Internal Auditing Policy, and Industrial Relations Policy. The Standards Manuals may be comprised of the following volumes: Quality Assurance Standards, Production Standards, Systems/Systems Tests Standards, Computer Operations Standards, Programming Coding Standards, Security Standards, and Documentation Standards. The set of Procedures Manuals may consist of: Clerical Procedures, Input/Output Procedures, Computer Operations/Run Books, Data Control Procedures, Training Procedures, and User's Guide.

NOTE: For a detailed discussion of the tasks and techniques that may be employed in writing a procedures manual, see Chapter 7.

1. POLICY MANUALS

Whether your project is to write a single policy manual or a set of manuals, the document(s) must convey the importance of adhering to the formulated policies for consistency in interpreting and administering top executive decisions. Written policies are also essential for clarifying procedural practices.

ESTABLISH RAPPORT WITH MANAGEMENT

A NOTE OF CAUTION: For successful completion of your project it is absolutely necessary to have rapport with top management and their immediate staff. Without their support and cooperation, writing a policy manual becomes an exercise in futility.

A single policy manual (for a medium or small company) should contain a description of all or most of the following topics:

1. Fixed company policies about hiring, vacations, pay periods, benefits, promotions, transfers, and terminations.

2. Circumstances in which supervisory personnel may make an exception to the established company policies in regard to a subordinate.

POLICIES THAT REFLECT MANAGEMENT ATTITUDES

3. Organizational structure of the firm and each department, to show the formulated chain of command.

4. Responsibilities and authority (job descriptions) of all levels of supervisory and professional positions.

5. Financial responsibilities of all levels of management in regard to the protection of company assets and resources.

6. Long and short range planning policies.
7. Merchandising policies.
8. Communications policies.
9. Purchasing policies.
10. Security and control policies.

a. **Writing the policy manual.** The format of this document(s) is comprised of the following:

Policy Manuals

CHIEF EXECUTIVE'S FOREWORD ADDS THAT "CERTAIN SOMETHING" TO A POLICY MANUAL

- Title page, table of contents, and foreword. Since at most enterprises the policy manual is a formal document, the title page and the table of contents/list of illustrations pages should be followed by a brief foreword from the chief executive. Most top executives are happy to oblige, especially if you write the foreword, and all he or she has to do is sign it.

- Introduction. In a policy manual the introduction is usually nothing more than a set of brief instructions on how to use the manual. It may also call attention to the fact that a simple method is provided to update the manual. (See Chapter 7 for a sample "Updating Log" and a description of the function of this form.)

- Organization chart. This diagram should display top management structure, and present how the communications lines—both up and down—are established. Putting it another way, an organization chart's function is to show who reports to whom in the hierarchy of corporate management. (See organization chart in Chapter 9, sample application, large and complex proposal.)

FOR GREATEST IMPACT USE SIMPLE, DIRECT STYLE IN THE BODY OF THE POLICY MANUAL

- Body. This is the main section of the policy manual. Here, according to predetermined priority you clarify in precise, direct language all the policies that top management decided upon and wishes to communicate to lower management. For ease of reference, there should be a subject index at the end of the manual.

NOTE: Since policy manuals are used for indoctrination of new employees as well as for everyday reference guides by all levels of management, the documents should be put in a sturdy, attractive binder, each section indicated by a laminated tab.

To provide an example of a policy manual, an abbreviated version of a description of Section 10 (listed earlier in this chapter) dealing with security and control policies follows.

SAMPLE Policy Manual

I. SECURITY AND CONTROL POLICIES

A. Introduction

It is the objective of this section to communicate and provide management policies for the protection and control of the Company's computing resources. To accomplish this objective, on the following pages we will:

- Define a system of control for all appropriate aspects of data protection.
- Provide a base for internal data protection audits.
- Define backup and recovery procedures to minimize the impact of accident, disaster, theft, or fraud.
- Establish guidelines for administration of the above program.

Resources that the established security measures are to protect include facilities, hardware/software, data, and personnel. The possible threats against these resources may be in the following areas:

- Errors and omissions.
- Accidents/disasters.
- Frauds.
- Strikes/sabotage.

The administration of these specific protection activities involve the following staff in the Company:

- **Directors.** They have the prime responsibility for securing and maintaining the protection of the Company's data resources, and for issuing appropriate procedures to obtain disciplined compliance with the established policies.
- **Managers.** They have the responsibility for preparing the appropriate plans; implementing the approved plans and controls; reporting irregularities; requesting assistance; and taking corrective actions.

I. Security and Control Policies

- **First level supervisors.** They (because they are in the best position to do so) have the responsibility to foster constructive attitudes toward security of data resources and compliance with management policies. Their responsibilities also include the detection and reporting of irregularities.
- **Quality assurance staff.** They have the responsibility to enforce the formulated security and control measures, and to review and certify new and/or modified computer systems and their documentation.
- **Facilities management.** They have the responsibility to carry out specific security/protection considerations.
- **Finance staff.** They have the responsibility to maintain financial control consistent with the state-of-the-art and with current Company policies.
- **Security staff.** They have the responsibility for security and fire protection, including physical control over access to the DP facility, internal security measures, and measures to safeguard classified and proprietary data. Their duties also include investigating all matters in which the interests of the Company might be placed in jeopardy or adversely affected, and certain aspects related to the employment, assignment, transfer, or termination of personnel.

B. Organization Control

To perpetrate computing fraud or theft requires availability of certain resources, such as:

- System knowledge, that is, in-depth understanding of how the particular system works.
- Access to the computer, that is, special password or other means of accessing the computer.
- Access to unique files, programs, or items through password or other means.
- A means of converting data or other computing resources to personal gain, such as setting up a fictitious client file.

A basic countermeasure is separation of duties, which in effect stops the perpetrator from accessing one or more of the items he or she needs. This forces the person into collusion with others, which significantly increases the difficulty of achieving the desired result. Intraorganizational separation of duties may also be employed to provide additional security measures. All systems involving resources are to be designed and operated so as to require double collusion to effect fraud. Systems such as sales, purchasing, payroll, accounts payable, accounts receivable, and so on, must be designed so that it would require triple collusion to effect fraud.

2. STANDARDS MANUALS

If written policies are essential for interpreting corporate decisions and organizational structures, and for clarifying procedural practices, written standards are imperative for uniformity of manual and computer data processing operations; for increasing overall efficiency; and for aiding communications between professional staff and line personnel.

EACH FUNCTION IN EACH DEPARTMENT NEEDS STANDARDS

Standards should be established in every department of an enterprise, especially the DP department. In point of fact no DP facility can run smoothly and efficiently without standards. Moreover, standards have to be defined and established before procedures can be developed.

ASSURE PERSONNEL THAT YOU'RE WORKING WITH THEM; NOT AGAINST THEM

NOTE: In developing standards and procedures manuals, it's very important to convince personnel from whom you are gathering data and who will have to follow the defined standards and procedures that you are working *with them* and *not against them*. Good relationships between you and your target readers will help the latter to follow the standards and procedures in your management approved documents.

a. **Writing the standards manual.** The format of this document(s) is comprised of the following:

- **Title page, table of contents/list of illustrations.** This manual too should have an attractive title page, and a table of contents/list of illustrations with wide margins.

- **Introduction.** As in the policy manual, this section provides brief instructions on how to use and update the manual.

STANDARDS FOR RELATED FUNCTIONS SHOULD BE CLUSTERED IN ONE MANUAL

- **Body.** Certain standards manuals such as security standards, quality control/assurance standards, and computer operations standards are usually separate documents. Standards for allied functions, however, are usually contained in one manual, with each function's standards separately defined. Standards for programming coding, Job Control Language (JCL), system and programming naming conventions, data element and data set naming conventions, for example, normally are included within one manual.

NOTE: Even though COBOL (Common Business Oriented Language), a standardized business programming language, has been around since 1961 when a committee sponsored by the U.S. Department of Defense and including representatives of large computer manufacturers issued specifications for COBOL, each DP facility still has to define and establish its unique COBOL standards. Moreover, before any computer system is designed or redesigned, developed, and implemented, it is absolutely necessary to define and establish standards for each phase. And while the actual coding of program logic does not start until the design phase is completed, the programming coding standards must be established concurrently with the system standards.

The following pages provide brief samples of standards for naming conventions, programming coding, and JCL conventions.

SAMPLE Standards for Naming Conventions

This section defines the standards for the naming conventions to be used by both Development and Operations personnel.

I. SYSTEM NAMING CONVENTIONS

The first three positions are reserved for the particular system's name, that is, its acronym or ID. The usage of this standard ensures uniformity for the computer system names.

Example: "INC" represents inventory control system.
"MOT" represents monthly totals system.

II. PROGRAM NAMING CONVENTIONS

1. Positions 1–3, XXX, represent the particular system's ID.
2. Positions 4–5, XX, represent the sequence of job within the system.
3. Positions 6–7, XX, represent the step number.
4. Position 8, X, represents the type of program, for example, U, S, E.

   Legend:
   - U   Update
   - E   Edit
   - S   Sort
   - B   Backup
   - R   Restore
   - Y   Utility
   - P   Reports

Example:
                    INC0512U
                    MOT1501S

III. JOB NAMES NAMING CONVENTIONS

1. Positions 1–3, XXX, represent the system's ID.
2. Position 4, X, represents location code, for example, A = Atlanta, C = Chicago.
3. Positions 5–6, XX, represent descriptive data, RN for RUN.
4. Positions 7–8, XX, represent the sequence of job within the system, for example, if there are 12 jobs within a system, positions 7–8 may be filled with a number from 01 to 12.

Example:

                        INCSRN09
                        MOTARN12

IV. STEP NAMES NAMING CONVENTIONS

1. Positions 1–3, XXX, represent the system's ID.
2. Positions 4–5, XX, represent the sequence of job within the system.
3. Positions 6–7, XX, represent the number relative to the step.
4. Position 8, X, represents the type of step, for example, P, U, S, E, and so on.

Example:

                        INC0125S
                        MOT0804E

V. PROCEDURES (PROC) NAMES NAMING CONVENTIONS

1. Positions 1–3, XXX, represent the particular system's ID.
2. Positions 4–5, XX, represent descriptive data.
3. Positions 6–7, XX, represent sequence of job within the system.
4. Position 8, X, indicates "P" for Proc.

Example:

                        INCRN09P
                        MOTRN12P

All jobs execute only *one Proc*. Moreover, the Proc name is the same as the job name.

VI. DATA DEFINITION NAMING CONVENTIONS

The data definition (DD) statement describes a data set to be used in a job step, and specifies the input and output facilities for the data set. Example:

//INCMSTR DD DSN = P.INC.N25S.P
(CARDID DD*, TAPE IN 1, DISKIN 1, DISKOUT 1, TAPEOUT1)

Where the DD name indicates Inventory Control Master; the DSN indicates Production; Inventory Control System; N, the job ID, and the 25S, the step ID.

VII. DATA SET NAMES NAMING CONVENTION

All data set names used for production or testing consist of four levels; generation data set names have a fifth level added by the System Catalog.

Levels are used in data set naming conventions so that data set names can exceed eight characters. This is possible because OS conventions allow up to 44 characters in a multilevel name. Levels extend from left to right, and are separated by a period ".". No spaces are allowed. For example, DSN = A.B.C., where A is the high level; B is the second level; and C is the third level in this 3-level data set name. In the case of generation data groups, the system adds an additional level in the form of "G0000V00," where the 4 zeroes following the "G" indicate the relative generation; while the 2 zeroes following the "V" indicate the version of this particular generation.

SAMPLE Programming Coding Standards

This section defines the standards for programming coding.

I. IDENTIFICATION DIVISION

The Identification Division must be included in every COBOL source program. It consists of the following:

IDENTIFICATION DIVISION.

PROGRAM-ID.	Program name and ID number.
AUTHOR.	The programmer's name.
DATE-WRITTEN.	Date the program is written.
REMARKS.	Describe the functions of the program and all the files used in the program. If the program is directly related to other programs or other systems, list their names and the program's relationship to them.

II. ENVIRONMENT DIVISION

The Environment Division must be included in every COBOL source program. It consists of the following:

ENVIRONMENT DIVISION.
CONFIGURATION SECTION.
INPUT-OUTPUT SECTION.
FILE-CONTROL.

III. DATA DIVISION

The Data Division must be included in every COBOL source program. It consists of the File, Working-Storage, Linkage, Communication, and Report Sections. There are many elements within these subsections. The Data Division's general format is:

DATA DIVISION.
FILE SECTION.
    (File-description-entry (record-description-entry)
    Sort-merge-file-description-entry (record description-entry))
WORKING-STORAGE SECTION.
    (77-level-description-entry
    Record-description-entry)
LINKAGE SECTION.
    (77-level-description-entry
    Record-description-entry)
COMMUNICATION SECTION.
    (Communication-description-entry (record-description-entry))
REPORT SECTION.
    (Report-description-entry (report-group-description-entry))

IV. PROCEDURE DIVISION

The Procedure Division must be included in every COBOL source program. This division consists of Housekeeping, Mainline Routine, Subroutines, and End-of-Job Routine. The Mainline Routine contains only general logic, and resides in front of the program. It should not be more than two pages of coding. The Mainline Routine should 'PERFORM' all needed functions in subroutines. Subsequently these subroutines may perform other lower-level subroutines.

    A procedure is composed of a paragraph, or group of paragraphs, or a section, or a group of sections within the Procedure Division. If one paragraph is in a section, then all paragraphs must be in sections. A procedure-name is a word that is used to refer to a paragraph or section in the source program in which it occurs. It consists of a paragraph-name (which may be qualified) or a section-name.

    A section consists of a section header, followed by zero, and one or more paragraphs. A paragraph consists of a paragraph-name, followed by a period and a space and a zero, and one or more sentences. A sentence consists of one or more statements, and is terminated by a period, followed by a space.

IV. Procedure Division

NOTE: 'GO TO' statements should be kept to a minimum. 'ALTER' statements must *not* be used. Switches should *not* be used.

Example:

```
PROCEDURE DIVISION.
    ENTRY 'RE31011A' USING LINKAGE-AREA.
A0010-TABLE-LOOKUP.
    .
    .
    .
    PERFORM A1110-FOUND THRU A1190-EXIT.
A0090-RETURN.
    GOBACK.

C0010-COMMON-ROUTINE.
    ENTRY 'RE31011C' USING LINKAGE-AREA.
    .
    .
    .
    PERFORM C1210-ROLL-TOTALS THRU C1290-EXIT.
    .
    .
    .
    PERFORM C2110-CREATE-EXTRACT-S120
                         THRU C2190-EXIT.
    .
    .
    .
C0090-RETURN.
    GOBACK
```

SAMPLE JCL Conventions Standards

Job Control Language (JCL) is the only way for an application program to first communicate with the operating system. In addition, it describes the work to be done by the system, that is, which program to execute, the sequence of execution, and the data sets required. Statements in JCL are used to identify specific functions to the operating system. The three basic JCL control statements are:

- Job statements.
- Execute statements.
- Data definition (DD) statements.

The fields in the control statements are:

- Name field.
- Operation field.
- Operand field.
- Comment field.

The different JCL types are:

JOB	Beginning of job
EXEC	Beginning of step
DD	Data definition
COMMAND	Operator command
NULL	End of JCL
DELIMITER	End of data
PROC	Beginning of procedures
PEND	End of procedures

Because it is vital in the maintenance phase of a system's life cycle that adding or modifying a program is done according to established standards, a System/Programming Standards manual is not complete without including a standard Service Request Form for program development/modification. Moreover, the form

IV. Procedure Division

should be followed by a detailed explanation of each statement on the form to ensure correct answers.

A sample service request form with a written account of each item on the form for program development or modification follows (Figure 39).

196 Writing Policy and Standards Manuals

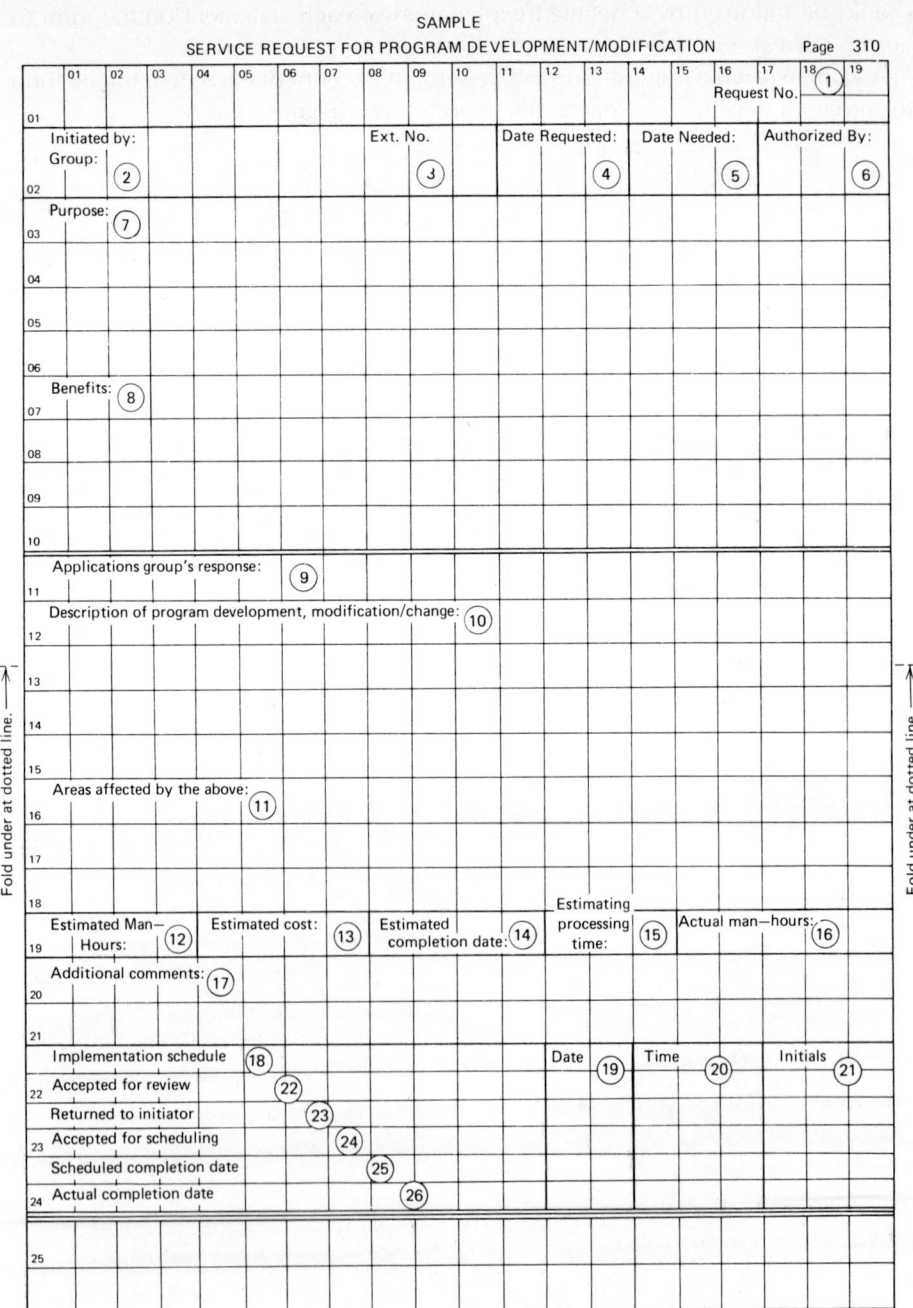

Figure 39. Sample: Service request for program development/modification.

SAMPLE Request for Program Development/Modification

This section defines the standards for conventions to be used in completing a Service Request for Program Development/Modification form.

1. This number is given by the Systems Development Section, and if the Service Request is approved, the same alpha-numeric is used all through the development as project ID.
2. Your name and group initiating the request.
3. Your extension number.
4. Date when you are preparing the service request.
5. Date when you need the requested service.
6. Signature or initials of person who is authorizing your request.
7. State briefly the purpose of your requested program development or modification/change.
8. State concisely the expected benefits of your requested program development or modification/change.
9. Beginning with this box, the form provides response of the Applications Group to the Service Request.
10. Delineate the requested project as proposed by your Applications Group.
11. Since it is imperative to know the particular areas that will be affected *before* starting on a new development, or modifying/changing currently running programs, list here those areas.
12. State estimated man-hours for the proposed project.
13. Determine estimated cost.
14. State estimated completion date.
15. State estimated processing time. (A more definitive projected processing time will be on Form 110.)
16. This box will be filled out after the project is accepted and completed.
17. Additional comments either by the initiator or the Applications Group.
18. The implementation schedule is presented in this section.
19. Dates for all possible actions in response to the Service Request.
20. The exact time of the response action.

21. Initials of the person(s) responsible for the particular action.
22. The date, time, and initials of person(s) accepting the Service Request for review.
23. The date, time, and initials of the person(s) returning the Service Request to the Initiator for a certain reason. For example, the requested modification is not feasible.
24. The date, time, and initials of the person(s) accepting the proposed project for scheduling.
25. The date, time, and initials of the person(s) scheduling the project's completion date.
26. This box will be filled out after the accepted project is implemented.

Chapter Eleven
Writing and Selling Technical Articles for Publication

"Put it before them *briefly* so they will read it; *clearly* so they will appreciate it; *picturesquely* so they will remember it; and above all *accurately* so they will be guided by its light."

This nearly century-old advice given to reporters by Joseph Pulitzer, publisher of *New York World*, is still appropriate not only to journalists but to DP professionals as well who want to see their name and articles in print, and get paid for it. Even publications that do not pay, such as *Communications of the ACM*, *ACM Computing Surveys*, and other similar professional and scientific association magazines insist on conciseness, clarity, and accuracy from their authors. Pedantic, verbose, slipshod, inaccurate articles won't sell in today's competitive technical publications market.

Consequently, writing a technical article involves much more than just sitting down and writing it, even if the subject is within your area of expertise. Writing is comprised of four distinct phases, each essential to produce a professional and salable product.

In this endeavor too, the preparatory phases take as much if not more effort and time than the actual writing of the article.

The four phases in creating a technical article for publication are the following:

1. Preliminary steps.
2. Cover or query letter.
3. Writing the article.
4. Editing the article.

1. PRELIMINARY STEPS

IT'S THE TOPIC THAT COUNTS

As in the case of material written for general category magazines, unless you can offer something new or something old with a new twist, inform, amaze, or entertain the audience, you don't have an article. For example, if you have been involved in the development of a novel software or application, or if you have reviewed and made copious notes of the new usage for a certain hardware (preferably field-tested), or if you have the answer as to how to solve a specific DP management problem, you have material for a technical article.

Once you have an interesting and/or informative idea for an article, the following steps should be taken.

LIGHTWEIGHT RESEARCH

a. **Perform cursory research.** Scan your notes, or gather enough informtion so that you can write an interesting and knowledgable outline and a lead paragraph that will grab the attention of the editor.

TIME-AND-EFFORT-SAVER OUTLINE

b. **Write an outline.** The outline for a technical article should be as compact as possible. If you can confine it to two, at the most three double-spaced pages, you can be sure that the editor will read it. An outline really serves two purposes: (1) to catch the editor's eye; and (2) to convince the editor that you have the necessary knowledge and background to write an authentic piece on whatever subject you are proposing. In addition, an outline in duplicate (original to the editor; copy for your files) saves you time and effort. You don't need to do in-depth research until you get the "go-ahead" from the editor—if you get it.

Moreover, at least you will get a fast reply, because a busy editor will read your brief outline before he or she will consider any manuscript of 5 to 15 pages. Thus, while a complete article may languish for a month or so in editorial offices before it is read, a decision to ask the author to write the article as indicated in the outline, or to reject the idea, is done far more rapidly. (A sample outline for a technical article follows.)

Preliminary Steps

NOTE: Once you have established yourself as a competent, reliable writer in certain publication(s), a telephone call to the editor(s) verbally outlining your topic is sufficient for him or her to give you the "go-ahead" on the article, or to decline your offer.

SAMPLE Outline for a Technical Article

Your Name
Your Address
Your Telephone No.

1. MINI-BASED LOGIC LETS USERS SOLVE PROBLEMS

By changing from manual office operations to an in-house minicomputer, a South San Francisco importer company has been able to reduce its inventory control work from 75 hrs/week to less than 4 hrs/week. Similarly, a Chicago accounting firm saved considerable turnaround time in its financial applications by switching from a service bureau to an in-house minicomputer.

    These dramatic reductions were effected by a new concept in small business computers: an integrated hardware/software minicomputer that allows nontechnical small business users to develop and execute business applications in English.

    When the management of the importer company—doing over $2 million business a year—decided to automate their manual processing, they investigated a number of systems. They finally chose EASY, a minicomputer with a built-in special software that the enterprise's nontechnical staff could program in English.

    Unlike the above company, the Chicago accounting firm has been using a computer service bureau for years to process their general ledger and financial statements. They were, however, unhappy with the 3 to 4 days delay in turnaround time. Moreover, because the service bureau did not have the capability to process corporate, business, and individual income tax returns, the accounting firm had to do them manually. Consequently, they looked into the possibility of eliminating the cost of the service bureau by having an in-house computer system that was affordable.

    These and other firms with divergent requirements and needs (to be detailed in the article) have been interviewed recently by me. With one exception, they all concurred that for their particular applications they were quite pleased with the total performance of this small, user-oriented business minicomputer.

    (An article by the author, based on this outline, appeared in the *Computerworld*.)

Preliminary Steps

STUDY SELECTED PUBLICATIONS

c. **Select and study the publications.** This step is essential not only to define the target readers of specific publication(s) that might be interested in your article, but also to determine the style and level of technical sophistication of the publication(s). By studying the content of a few issues of a magazine you can easily determine the type of readers the particular publication is targeting. For example, the style and level of technical sophistication of DATAMATION magazine that aims at management-oriented DP professional readers is quite different from PERSONAL COMPUTING magazine, which directs its content at home and small business computer users. That, however, does not mean that the same topic is not suitable for several technical publications. It is the language, the point of view, the depth of details, and the type of presentation that makes the difference.

For your information a partial list of technical publications, their addresses, and their target readers follows:

BYTE MAGAZINE, 70 Main St., Peterborough, NH 03458. Publishes articles on personal microcomputers.

COMPUTER DECISION, 50 Essex St., Rochelle Park, NJ 07662. Publishes articles for MIS/DP managers on making decisions about computer acquisitions and applications.

COMPUTER BUSINESS NEWS, 375 Cochituate Rd., Framingham, MA 01701. Publishes articles for dealers, distributors, original equipment manufacturers (OEM), and other multiple-unit buyers of computer products and services.

COMPUTERWORLD, 375 Cochituate Rd., Framingham, MA 01701. Publishes articles for DP professionals and management-level computer users in the business community and in government.

CREATIVE COMPUTING, P.O. Box 789-M, Morristown, NJ 07960. Publishes articles on the educational and recreational applications of computers, the effects of computers on society, and the building of computers at home.

DATA COMMUNICATIONS, McGraw-Hill Bldg., 1221 Avenue of the Americas, New York, NY 10020. Publishes articles for professional people responsible for the use, planning, design, and implementation of data communications systems in business, industry, and government.

DATAMATION, 1301 So. Grove Ave., Barrington, IL 60010. Publishes articles for management-oriented DP professionals.

INFOSYSTEMS, Hitchcock Bldg., Wheaton, IL 60187. Publishes articles on DP management, computer applications, and so on, related to banking.

PERSONAL COMPUTING. 50 Essex St., Rochelle Park, NJ 07662. Publishes articles on home and small business uses of computers, techniques, games, product reviews, interviews, and programs.
programs.

POPULAR ELECTRONICS, One Park Ave., New York, NY 10016. Publishes articles on computers, consumer electronics technology, and so on.

WORDS MAGAZINE, IWP, Old York Rd., Willow Grove, PA 19090. The Journal of the International Word Processing Association. Publishes articles for word processing managers, consultants, and vendors.

2. **COVER OR QUERY LETTER**

a. **The cover letter** that accompanies the outline is really nothing more than your asking the editor to take a speculative look at the attached outline, as well as introducing yourself to him or her. To enforce the impression that your proposed article will be accurate and authoritative, you should state your qualifications and, if you have had any articles published, the magazines in which they appeared. This applies whether you are writing a cover letter or a query letter.

A cover letter that is sent along with your outline might read: "Would you be interested in receiving a 2,000 word article based on the attached outline for possible publication?

"I'm a DP Management Consultant in the areas of data communications networks and MIS. Prior to going into consulting, I was MIS Manager at CAS Inc., Dallas, TX, for five years. I hold an M.S. in Computer Science from the University of Chicago, and a B.S. in Mathematics from U.C.L.A. Articles by me have appeared in Data Communications and Computer Decision.''

b. The query letter incorporates the outline and the cover letter. Because of its strict requirements and format, perhaps even more thought and effort have to go into a query letter than into an outline. There are many pros and cons about outlines versus query letters.

Those who favor approaching the editor via an outline plus a cover letter point out that:

PROS FOR OUTLINE/W COVER LETTER

- Having a brief cover letter introduce the outline and present the qualifications of the author favorably "conditions" the editor toward the proposed article.
- If the editor rejects the proposed topic, he or she returns the outline, usually with accompanied comments. This, of course, means that if an outline is rejected, you don't have to do a lot of retyping when approaching another editor. The only thing you have to retype is the cover letter.

On the other hand, DP professionals who insist on approaching the editor via a query letter say that:

PROS FOR QUERY LETTER

- Editors, in general, much prefer to read a one or at the most two page query letter rather than two or three pages of outline plus a cover letter.
- Editors appreciate your stating succinctly in a few paragraphs the topic, the theme, and the approach of your proposed article. A query letter is enough for them to make a decision, and it saves them valuable time.

In any case, an effective query letter arouses the interest of the editor in the first word, first sentence, first paragraph. This is followed by two or three brief paragraphs of the bare-bone outline of your proposed article. And the letter ends with your qualifications and credits, if you have any.

AN IMPORTANT POINT

NOTE: Whereas the outline is always presented to the editor double-spaced, with wide margins around the typed text, the cover and query letters are single-spaced, with double spaces between the paragraphs. Whether you indent or use the block format, however, there should be wide margins around the typed text in the letters also.

Writing an effective cover letter can be a problem. To assist you in this difficult task, a sample query letter is presented on the next page.

SAMPLE: Query Letter

Date

Editor's Name and Title
Publication's Name
Publication's Address

Dear _____:

Security! With the burgeoning of distributed data processing and data communications networks, security, following closely after data integrity and reliability, is one of the crucial problems that DP management has to deal with currently. While security is quite important in centralized data bases, they do not have the special problems that are posed in DDP and DC networks. Consequently, such traditional security measures as the periodic changing of passwords and IDs, for example, are not sufficient in the latter environments against today's sophisticated white-collar computer criminals.

Would you care to see, for possible publication, a 2000 to 2500 word article that presents the latest field-tested security techniques and controls that can be implemented at large as well as medium-sized facilities? The techniques discussed are designed to guard against, or at least minimize computer fraud, unauthorized use of the system, and so on.

I'm a Senior Computer Security Analyst with Computer Research Institute, Princeton, N.J. I also lecture at various colleges and professional symposiums. I received my B.S. in Computer Science from M.I.T.

Sincerely,

John Smythe
533 Hobart Avenue
Princeton, NJ 07662

Enc: Self-addressed stamped envelope

PUBLISHED OR NOT—QUERY THE EDITOR

NOTE: Unlike the majority of general magazines, technical publications don't hold it against you if you can't list credits in other magazines. If the subject is interesting, they will ask to see it. And if the resulting article is well-written and accurate, they will buy it and publish it. In other words, if you have material for an interesting and/or informative article, even if you have never sold anything before, do query an editor. If your outline or query letter presents your topic in a professional manner, and if you have appropriate qualifications, you have just as much chance as anybody else to have your material considered by the editor.

The best outline or query letter, however, does not guarantee that the editor will give you the "go-ahead" to write the article. He or she might turn it down for many reasons, such as: he or she published a piece on the same subject recently; he or she doesn't think the piece would interest the magazine's target readers; the topic is too technical for his or her readers; the topic is not technical enough for the readers, and so on.

If your idea is rejected, don't get discouraged; don't give up; query another technical publication editor.

IF YOUR ARTICLE IS REJECTED

It can also happen that the article—after the query was given a speculative affirmative reply—is rejected. This occurs when the finished article doesn't live up to its previous billing. If your article is rejected, critique it as objectively as possible, and if necessary edit it. Then query another technical publication editor either about the same version, or perhaps the same article but with a different slant. It just might be the exact article the editor needs for the next issue of his/her magazine.

c. **Acknowledge the editor's response.** If the editor answers your query with "Yes, I would be glad to see your article on speculation," before you plunge into the research and writing phases, take a few minutes and acknowledge his or her response. Not only is this the courteous and professional thing to do, but it informs the editor when to expect the manuscript.

In your enthusiasm, however, don't make the mistake of underestimating the time it will take you to produce the article. Rather, give yourself a margin of safety and add 25% to any estimate. If, for example, you estimate that it will take you four weeks to check your facts, do in-depth research, write and edit your article, and draw the schematics (if you feel that they will add to your presentation, or if the editor asks you to illustrate it), add at least another week.

"COOL" YOUR ARTICLE FOR A WHILE

In case you can mail it earlier, the editor will be pleased. But if you send your article later than you promised, the displeased editor may reject it, or he/she may never buy another article from you. Besides, by giving yourself extra time, you will be able, after completing the article, to "cool it," that is, to put it away for a few days before you edit it. It's amazing how many mistakes (spelling, typos, redundancy) one discovers in an article that a few days before was thought to be perfect.

3. WRITING THE ARTICLE

a. **Lead.** If the editor liked your query or outline, it's a safe bet to start your article with the proposed lead intact, or perhaps with only a slight modification.

ACCENTUATE THE POSITIVE

b. **Audience.** As you write the article keep your intended audience constantly in mind. Thus, if you are writing an article from the non-DP user's viewpoint, for example, don't switch to the systems designer or programmer's viewpoint, or you'll lose your reader, not to mention the editor. And above all, regardless of who your audience is, do not dwell on the negative aspects of the stated problem or subject but emphasize how the problem was resolved, or is planned to be resolved.

MATCH THE LANGUAGE AND STYLE TO YOUR READERS

c. **Style and language.** If your article is going to a publication that caters to DP management or other nonprogramming users, describe your topic in nontechnical language and use conversational style. Similarly, if you are discussing a high technology topic for sophisticated DP professionals, describe your topic in technical language and use formal yet clear and fluent style. Watch out that in the former piece you don't switch from conversational style and nontechnical language to formal style and technical language, and that in the latter article you don't do the opposite.

OBSERVE THE MECHANICS OF CLEAR WRITING

The mechanics of clear writing (Chapter 2) certainly apply to the creating of technical articles. Putting it another way, regardless of who your audience is, from nontechnical people to top-level technical individuals, you should: employ specific, concrete, and vivid language; use adjectives and adverbs selectively; vary the length of sentences and paragraphs to keep the audience's interest; and check that your transitions (from one sentence to another, from one paragraph to another) are smooth and appropriate.

Strive for a single effect. Make every sentence and paragraph contribute to the total impression. Stimulate your readers to mental and/or physical responses such as implementing some of your suggestions, investigating the software or hardware you are discussing, and so on.

Finally, if it's important for your opening sentence to be an attention-grabber, it's just as important that your closing sentence leaves the reader satisfied. In other words, make your conclusion short and sweet.

An excellent example of an interesting lead is that of P. G. Elam, Cincom Systems, Inc., Cincinnati, in his published article, "Considering Human Needs Can Boost Network Efficiency."*

Mr. Elam opens his article with:

*EXECUTIVE GUIDE TO DATA COMMUNICATIONS, Vol. 30, 1980. McGraw-Hill Publications Company, New York, NY.

Editing the Article

SPECIFIC EXAMPLES

> Although interactive systems bring tremendous power to the fingertips of data processors—almost instantaneous responses to questions about personnel, budgets, or raw material for technicians or department managers—that very power may be intimidating enough to cause users to shy away from such systems.

He concludes his article with:

> But, most important, poor design causes the user to become frustrated. And the frustrated user tends not to use the system.

Another example of effective lead and closing sentences can be found in K. A. Parker's article, "Productivity at Heart of DBMS Question."* Mr. Parker's opening sentence is:

> The clear challenge for the DP community is productivity—increasing the usable output from the available resources.

The article ends with:

> If DBMS will not increase people productivity and provide greater and more responsive user service, it is not for you.

4. EDITING THE ARTICLE

Because editing and/or rewriting an article is a tedious job at best, many people are reluctant to attend to this task. That is a mistake that can cost you the sale of your article.

a. Irrelevant data. To ensure that every single detail, and/or data and information included in the written piece is pertinent to your topic, go over your article with the proverbial fine-tooth comb. There may be a temptation to include all the data and information you have gathered in your research. However, for the sake of a single effect in your article, you must resist this temptation and ruthlessly cut out everything that is not relevant. A lean article is much more forceful than one from which the literary fat has not been trimmed.

---

*Copyright 1979 CW Communications Inc., Framingham, MA 01701. Reprinted from COMPUTERWORLD.

PRESENT YOUR ARTICLE IN A PROFESSIONAL FORMAT

b. Format. Besides double-spacing and using wide margins—1½ inch on top; 1¼ inch on the left; 1 inch on the right and on the bottom of the typewriter paper—you should employ frequent headings in your text to punctuate the important points. Don't forget to put your name, address, and phone number (single-spaced) on the top left-hand corner of the first page, and the approximate number of words that the article contains on the top right-hand corner of the first page. (See the sample professional format for an article manuscript at the end of this chapter.) Also, number your pages—on the upper right-hand corner—beginning with page 2.

An article does not need a title page or a binder. Only neophytes think that such practice contributes to the acceptability of their manuscript. The fact is that it creates just the opposite effect on the editor. Besides, with today's high postage rates, an article in a binder, even if it's lightweight, will cost you at least three times as much as if you mail your manuscript (folded) in a regular business envelope. Even so, a 2,000 word article, for example, will end up as eight or nine double-spaced, typed pages, not counting the accompanying letter plus the folded self-addressed stamped envelope (SASE) for possible return of the article. Thus, it will cost you a dollar or more. If you intend to write more articles, or if you have to send out the same article to half a dozen publications, it adds up.

c. Spelling and typos. Nothing turns off an editor faster than incorrect spelling and/or poorly typed manuscript. If spelling is not one of your strong points, type your article with a dictionary at your elbow. Also, watch out for typos.

If you cannot type a page without a half a dozen or so typos, which you then try to erase or cover with correction liquid, perhaps you should have a professional secretary/typist do that task. But whether you or somebody else types the mail-off copy of your article, you should proofread it very carefully. Nobody is infallible, and the best of typists can make a mistake or two.

d. Accompanying letter. The letter that is attached to your article should be as brief as possible. You might say: "Per our correspondence, enclosed please find my article, _____, _____ words approx., for your consideration." Then sign it, adding underneath "Encs: Manuscript and SASE."

Do not repeat anything that you have said in your previous cover or query letter, and do not say, "I have worked very hard on the enclosed article," or "I hope you like my article." Such things are dead giveaways of a novice. If your article and accompanying letter are professional, the editor will treat you accordingly.

SAMPLE Format for the First Page of an Article

Your Name
Your Address
Your Phone No.
———words approx.

                    TITLE
TEXT

1¼ in. margin   1 in. margin

1 in. margin

Index

Acronyms:
   defining, 15
   use, 21–22
Activity table, 68–73
Adjectives, selective use, 14–15
Adverbs, selective use of, 14–15
Ambiguity, 15
Applications and maintenance programmers, information geared to, 28, 29, 30
Appointments, scheduling for interview, 39
Audience, *see* Target readers, defining

Betanet system, procedures to, 113–114
"Bottom-up" approach, to data collection, 38
Byte Magazine, 204

Charts, *see* Graphics
Chronological sequence, data organized in, 42, 45
Clear writing, 2–3, 13
   communication needed for, 17
   conciseness for, 20
   direct language use, 18–20
   editing for, 22–23
   personal viewpoint used for, 20–21
   principles of, 14–16
   purpose of writing and, 18
COBOL, standards for, 187
Coding, sample of standards for programming, 191–193
Computer Business News, 203
Computer Decision, 203
Computerworld, 203
Conceptual flowchart, 54, 56
Conciseness, 20
Conclusion, of progress report, 95–96, 101
Content format standards, 50, 52

Control and security, *see* Security and control
Conventions, sample of standards for naming, 186–190
Correspondence, data collection from, 37
Cost analysis:
   of feasibility study, 126, 128, 140
   of technical proposal, 31, 152, 162–163
Cover letter, for technical article for publication, 204–205, 206
   see also Transmittal letter, of technical proposal
Creative Computing, 203
Critical Path Method (CPM), 68, 70–71
   chart of, 176

Data collection, 37–38
   organizing, 42–46
Data Communications, 203–204
Datamation, 204
Decision table, 66
Design specifications, sample of, 141–143
Detailed outline, 49–50
Diagrams, 65
Discriminative writing, 14–15
Discussion:
   of feasibility study, 128, 133–134
   of progress report, 95, 99–101
   of technical proposal, 31
Documentation techniques:
   HIPO, 6, 53, 76–81
      samples, 77–78, 80, 81–82, 84, 86
   SADT, 6, 53, 69, 75, 81, 84
      samples, 82, 83, 85

Editing, 22–23
Examples, supplying, 16

Index

Executive summary, of large technical proposal, 161, 168–169
Exhibits, 74–76

Flowchart, 54–64, 135
  for feasibility study, 126
Follow-up/updating method, for writing procedures, 107–108
Formal small technical proposal, 149–151, 152–159
Functional flowchart, 57, 60

General system flowchart, 57, 58, 59
Glossary, for writing procedures, 107
Graphics, 5–6, 53
  charts:
    diagrams, 65
    flowcharts, 54–64, 135
    exhibits, 74–76
    tables, 66–73
  see also Documentation techniques

Hardware configurations flowchart, 57, 62
Hierarchical order presentation, of data organization, 42, 44
Hierarchy plus Input, Process, and Output (HIPO), *see* Documentation techniques
HIPO, *see* Documentation techniques

Illustrations, *see* Documentation techniques; Graphics
Illustrations list:
  of feasibility study, 131
  of formal small technical proposal, 155
  of large technical proposal, 167
  of progress report, 92–93
Informal small technical proposal, 151
Information, *see* Data Collection
Infosystems, 204
Initials, use of, 21–22
Input-processing section, for nontechnical users, 30
Interviews:
  data collection from, 38
  prior to writing, 38–41
Introduction:
  of feasibility report, 127, 133
  of large technical proposal, 160–161, 168
  of policy manual, 183, 184
  of progress report, 94–95, 99

Job Control Language (JCL), sample of conventions standards for, 194–196
Job descriptions, data collection from, 38
Job step flowchart, 57, 63, 117

Language, use of direct, 18–19
Layout format standards, 50–51
Logic flowchart, 57, 61, 136

Mail room, procedures for, 111, 115–116, 120, 121–122
Management, writing to, 31–32
Management overview, of a proposal, 30–31
Manloading/scheduling table, 66, 67
Manuals, 9, 181
  policy manuals, 182–184
    sample, 184–185
  standards manual, 186–187
  samples, 18
  see also Procedures
"Marketing myopia," 26–27

Nontechnical applications users, information geared to, 28, 29, 30
Nouns, verbs turned into, 15

Objectives:
  defining and establishing, 36
  of feasibility report, 127, 131
  technical proposal and, 150, 156–157
Operations manual, positions requiring, 29
Opinions, during interview, 40
Organization chart:
  data collection from, 37
  in policy manual, 183
Outline:
  prior to writing report, 47–50
  for publishing a technical article, 200–202, 205, 206, 208

Peers, writing to, 32
Personal Computing, 204
PERT (Project Evaluation Review Technique), 68, 72–73
Picture pattern, for procedures, 119–120
Place order presentation, of data organization, 42–43, 46–47
Plan, prior to writing, 4–5, 35–36
  content format standards, 50, 52
  data collection, 37–38

Index

data organization, 42–46
interviews, 38–41
layout format standards, 50–51
outlining of material, 47–50
personality of document determination, 47
project definition, 36–37
software check, 42
summarizing document content, 50
Playscript pattern, for procedures, 120–122
Policy, data collection from corporate, 37
Policy manual, 182–184
sample, 184–185
Popular Electronics, 204
Preparation for writing, *see* Plan, prior to writing
Pricing schedule, of technical proposal:
of formal small, 151
of large complex, 162–163
see also Cost analysis
Prior to writing, *see* Plan, prior to writing
Problem, statement of:
in feasibility report, 127, 132–133
in technical proposal, 150, 156
Procedures, 7, 103–104, 181
data collection from, 37
final copy, 107
follow-up/updating method, 107–108
formats:
picture pattern, 119–120
playscript pattern, 120–122
text-flowchart pattern, 114–119
text pattern, 109–114
preliminary steps/considerations, 104–107
sign-off/approval, 109
Professional nontechnical applications users, information geared to, 28, 29, 30
Program development/modification, sample of standards for contentions used in, 197–198
Progress reports, 6–7, 89
conclusion, 95–96
discussion, 95
front section, 90–93
introduction, 94–95
sample, 99–101
summary, 93–94
Project, defining, 36–37
Project Evaluation Review Technique (PERT), 68, 72–73
Proposal, *see* Technical proposal

Public, writing to, 33
see also Publication, technical article prepared for
Publication, technical article prepared for, 33, 199
cover letter for, 204–205, 206
cursory research, 200
editing, 211–213
first page format, 214
letter accompanying, 213
outline for, 200–202, 205
publications studied, 203–204
query letter for, 205, 206, 207–208
rejection of, 208–209
writing, 209–214
Publications, in data processing, 203–204

Query letter, for technical article for publication, 205, 206, 207–208

Reader, consideration of before products, 26–27
see also Target reader, defining
Reader-oriented communications, 26–27
Redundancy, eliminating, 14
Request for Proposal (RFP), 147
see also Technical proposal
Request for Quotation (RFQ), 147
see also Technical proposal
RFP (Request for Proposal), 147, 150, 160
see also Technical proposal
RFQ (Request for Quotation), 147
see also Technical proposal
Runbook, *see* Operations manual

SADT, *see* Documentation techniques
Schedule:
establishing tentative, 37
of interviewee, 39
Scope of project, setting, 36
Security and control:
in feasibility study, 126, 128, 138–139
sample policy manual on, 184–186
Skeletal outline, 48–49
Software, checking:
prior to report-writing, 42
for procedures, 105
Spatial order presentation, of data organization, 42–43, 46–47
Standards, for procedures, 105–106

Standards manual, 186–187
  samples, 188–198
Status report, 89
  see also Progress reports
Structure Analysis and Design Technique (SADT), *see* Documentation techniques
Subordinates, writing to, 33
Summary:
  of document content, 50
  executive, 161, 168–169
  of feasibility study, 127, 131
  of progress report, 93–94, 99
Summary outline, 48
System and programming manual, positions requiring, 29
Systems analysts/designers, information geared to, 28, 29, 30
Systems programmers, information geared to, 28, 29, 30
Systems study:
  design specifications sample, 141–143
  feasibility study, 7–8, 123–124
    contents, 127–128
    definition, 123
    for entire organization, 123
    for particular department, 123
    planning, 124–126
    sample, 129–140
    writing, 126–127

Table of contents:
  of feasibility study, 127, 130
  of formal small technical proposal, 155
  of large technical proposal, 167
  of progress report, 91–92, 98
Tables, 66–73
Tape recording, of interview, 40
  transcribing, 41
Target readers, defining, 3–4, 14, 25, 27
  interest level of reader aimed at, 28–31
  management written to, 31–32
  peers written to, 32
  procedures matched for, 106
  project definition and, 36–37
  public written to, 33, 209–210. *See also* Publication, technical article preparation for
  reader-oriented communications, 26–27
  subordinates written to, 33
Task and time schedules, for large technical proposal, 177
Technical applications users, information geared to, 28, 29
Technical approach of technical proposal:
  of formal small, 157–158
  of large, 162, 172–174
Technical discussion, *see* Discussion
Technical proposal, 147–148
  defining readers for, 30–31
  large and complex proposal, 160–163
    sample, 164–179
  proposal committee, 147
  small and simple proposal, 148
    formal and sample, 149–151, 152–153
    informal, 151
Text-flowchart pattern, for procedures, 114–119
Time-order presentation, of data organization, 42, 45
Title page:
  of feasibility study, 127, 129
  of formal, small technical proposal, 154
  of large, technical proposal, 166
  of progress report, 90–91, 97
"Top-down" approach, to data collection, 37–38
Transcribing, of the interview, 41
Transmittal letter, of technical proposal:
  of formal, small, 149–150
  of large, complex, 164–165

Updating log, 107–108
User's guide, positions requiring, 29

Verbiage, unnecessary, 14
Verbs:
  active *vs.* passive, 15–16
  nouns from, 15
  tenses, 16
Viewpoint, impersonal *vs.* personal, 20–21

Words Magazine, 204
Work flowchart, 57, 64